GETTING IT Wrong

FROM THE BEGINNING

GETTING IT wrong

FROM THE BEGINNING

Our Progressivist Inheritance
from Herbert Spencer, John Dewey,
and Jean Piaget

KIERAN EGAN

Yale University Press New Haven & London

Set in Minion type by The Composing Room of Michigan, Inc.,
Grand Rapids, Michigan.
Printed in the United States of America by Vail-Ballou Press,
Binghamton, New York.

Library of Congress Cataloging-in-Publication Data

Egan, Kieran.
Getting it wrong from the beginning : our progressivist inheritance
from Herbert Spencer, John Dewey, and Jean Piaget / Kieran Egan.
  p.   cm.
Includes bibliographical references (p.   ) and index.
ISBN 0-300-09433-7 (clothbound : alk. paper)
1. Education—United States—Philosophy.   2. Progressive
education—United States—History.   3. Spencer, Herbert, 1820–
1903—Influence.   4. Dewey, John, 1859–1952.   5. Piaget, Jean,
1896– .   I. Title.
LA212 .E53   2002
370'.1—dc21   2001008389

A catalogue record for this book is available from the British
Library.

The paper in this book meets the guidelines for permanence and
durability of the Committee on Production Guidelines for Book
Longevity of the Council on Library Resources.

10 9 8 7 6 5 4 3 2 1

To

Michael James Egan

with love

CONTENTS

Acknowledgments *ix*

Introduction *1*

Chapter 1
The Strange Case of Herbert Spencer *11*

Chapter 2
Learning According to Nature's Plan *37*

Chapter 3
Development, Progress, and the Biologized Mind *79*

Chapter 4
The Useful Curriculum *115*

Chapter 5
Research Has Shown That . . . *149*

Conclusion *183*

References *187*

Index *199*

ACKNOWLEDGMENTS

I have been fortunate to receive comments on the manuscript of this book and suggestions for its improvement from a number of kind and incisively critical people. Jack Martin and Jeff Sugarman, colleagues at Simon Fraser University, have been generous with their time and suggestions, for which I am grateful. Also generous has been John Willinsky, at the University of British Columbia—though his help came more from chatting about the ideas of the book while he hefted stones and moved earth while helping me build my Japanese garden. Two teachers, administrators, and scholars who have been graciously helpful over the years have also contributed: it is a pleasure to acknowledge Apko Nap in British Columbia and Marc Heller in Connecticut.

While writing the book, I had the good fortune to discuss its arguments with Natalia Gajdamashko, a visiting scholar at Simon Fraser University. I value her suggestions for improving the book, especially with regard to Lev Vygotsky's work, but also with regard to a range of theoretical issues. Hannah Gay, of Simon Fraser University's history department, has kindly read the chapter on Herbert Spencer and made suggestions that have improved it considerably, though she mustn't be blamed for its remaining insufficiencies.

Grants from the Social Sciences and Humanities Research Council of Canada and the Spencer Foundation have enabled me to travel to conferences to present some of the ideas in the book and receive useful criticisms.

These generous grants also allowed me time for writing and paid for graduate assistance. Cliff Falk and Jan Bonzon provided exten-sive and insightful comments on the manuscript. The student whose daunting assiduousness and energetic and intelligent help is mentioned in the text is Emery Hyslop-Margison, who deserves special thanks.

Susan Arellano, my initial editor at Yale University Press, helped me wrestle with the monstrous manuscript that is now to appear as two separate books, this being the first. I would like to record my gratitude for her insight and humor and lots of good advice. Laura Jones Dooley of Yale University Press has smoothed the narrative that lies ahead, for which I am—and no doubt you are—most grateful.

Devi Pabla and Eileen Mallory turned my scrawling handwrit-ing into immaculate typescript. Just as the typescript was com-pleted, Eileen Mallory retired—not, I hope, a causal connection. She has typed more words of mine that either of us cares to remem-ber, and indeed, I feel by now that I need only mention a topic and she could probably write the book without me. I have been happy to acknowledge her help in nearly all my previous books, and it is with real sadness that I make this, probably last, printed expression of heartfelt thanks.

GETTING IT Wrong
FROM THE BEGINNING

INTRODUCTION

Imagine it is the year 1887 and you are a forty-five-year-old white middle-class man traveling by train into a medium-sized American town. You would likely see some new buildings going up. Perhaps the biggest is a factory, and nearby are the shells of houses for the workers, and perhaps a new church and school are being built. You are financially comfortable and aware that your personal wealth and that of your neighbors is growing as a direct or indirect result of the products of the new factories and the trade they generate. The town's population is increasing, there are more, and more varied, shops and services, and new inventions are transforming your life.

Let us say you know that the factory under construction, which you are turning to look at as you pass by, will make equipment for the new electric lighting system. Your home is now lighted by gas, with a few older kerosene lamps for use in upstairs rooms. You would know that a decade ago Sir Joseph Wilson Swan had invented a new incandescent lamp by heating carbon filaments in a glass bulb from which air was partially evacuated. In the following year, Thomas Alva Edison came up with the same idea, but unlike the Englishman, Edison developed plans for the power lines and equipment needed to establish a practical lighting system. You can foresee this new electric light replacing the less safe, less clean, and less efficient system you now use.

All this change, these buildings and inventions, the growing town and shifting patterns in people's lives, you recognize, somewhat proudly, as progress. Being a progressive modern man you have learned the ideas propounded by other white middle-class men during the past half-century or so. Unlike all your ancestors, and unlike all people in other than modern Western societies, you confidently believe that the world developed from a mass of molten matter to its present life-supporting form, that life itself evolved from the simplest bugs to that pinnacle of life on the planet—yourself—and that civilizations have similarly evolved from primitive beginnings to the inventive sophistication of your own. This social evolution from primitive to modern societies, you recognize, has not, of course, been uniform; many societies remain in a developmentally "primitive" condition, still living a life reflective of "the childhood of mankind." You understand the now-common phrase "the childhood of mankind" as capturing the sense in which "primitive" people's minds are inferior to your modern mind much as children's minds are inferior to those of adults.

As a progressive modern man you will have read the celebrated and influential essay written thirty years ago by Herbert Spencer called "Progress: Its Law and Cause." Spencer had persuaded you, and many others, that "progress is not an accident, not a thing within human control, but a beneficent necessity" (Spencer 1966, 60). He had established that this underlying law was "displayed in the progress of civilization as a whole, as well as in the progress of every nation; and is still going on with increasing rapidity" (19). That factory, those new houses, and the train you are riding in are all confirming evidence of his compelling argument.

As your train carries you on, at a speed and with a comfort unimaginable to any traveler before you in history, you recognize that the physical and social changes you see are reflected in, or are products of, a ferment of new ideas. The number and novelty of these new ideas is disruptive on a scale never before experienced. The result creates anxiety in those who see the foundations of their old intellectual world being threatened but is exhilarating to progressive minds like yours.

Let us say, as you passed that school being built, you turned to look at it with a particular and professional interest because you are a recently appointed senior official of this newly organized school division. The ferment of ideas you are aware of will prominently include those about education. You hold decided ideas about how the new state schools should go about educating all the children in society for the New World. The new world that is tangibly coming into form around you would be the world they will inhabit, and you are keenly aware that it will be quite unlike the world you grew up in. Your educational ideas have also been influenced by the redoubtable Mr. Spencer, an Englishman born in 1820 who has written at length about education, as he has written about nearly every other topic a modern man might turn his mind to. Spencer made a triumphant lecture tour around America in 1882, and, let us say, you attended two of his exciting talks. His ideas about education draw on the same fundamental principles that undergird his progressive arguments about the development of life, of civilization, and of individuals' potential.

Well, let us imagine now that you are you—a tougher call, perhaps—and consider our man on the train from the outside. He was an agent in creating the kind of schools we still have. He, and hundreds like him, shaped the new schools under the influence of a set of powerful educational ideas. During the late nineteenth century, the modern apparatus for schooling everyone was put in place. My topic is the ideas about education that shaped these new state schools into the forms we have lived with ever since, and particularly the ideas about children's minds, and their modes of learning and development, which have determined the curriculum and the organization of schools.

In the 1850s, Herbert Spencer wrote four essays on education. They were published separately in journals, but he had intended from the beginning that they would appear as a single volume. That volume was published in New York under the title *Education: Intellectual, Moral, and Physical* in 1860 and in London the following year. By the end of the 1860s the book had appeared in fifteen editions from seven publishers. During the 1870s it was reprinted in New York nine times by D. Appleton alone, and in the 1880s there were fifteen printings, all but two in the United States. (The laxness of copyright laws, especially concerning foreign publications, helps account for this proliferation.) In the 1890s, it seems, a slowdown in popularity occurred, with only thirteen printings during the decade, including editions from seven American publishers. Appleton itself sold hundreds of thousands of copies.

The later nineteenth century was a crucial period for educational thinking. Rapid population growth, industrial development, and the beginnings of universal schooling coincided with reverberations from the stunning theory of evolution. Herbert Spencer stood at this crux. He drew on a range of new ideas and shaped a set of educational principles that became and have remained fundamental in the thinking of those who have had responsibility for our schools, even if their historical source has become invisible to those who hold them.

The historian of education Lawrence Cremin has described the 1890s as revolutionary for American education. He cites the influential books that appeared in that decade, including William James's *Principles of Psychology* in 1890 and his *Talks to Teachers on Psychology* in 1899, Francis W. Parker's *Talks on Pedagogics* in 1894, Edward L. Thorndike's *Animal Intelligence* in 1898, and John Dewey's *School and Society* in 1899. Cremin might have extended his time frame a little to include G. Stanley Hall's two-volume *Adolescence: Its Psychology and Its Relations to Physiology, Anthropology, Sociology, Sex, Crime, Religion, and Education* in 1904. These "revolutionaries" had in common the fact that they were all profoundly influenced by Spencer's work: "If the revolution had a beginning, it was surely with the work of Herbert Spencer" (Cremin 1961, 91). In the generation after Spencer's death, it was uncontentious to claim for the collection of educational essays he wrote that "more than any other single text-book it is the foundation of all the so-called 'modern' ideas in education" (Samuel and Elliot 1917, 176).

"By the 1950s," Cremin has also claimed, "the more fundamental tenets of the progressives had become the conventional wisdom of American education" (1976, 19). And many people today assert that our schools' ineffectiveness is due precisely to the influence of these progressivist ideas. But those sympathetic to progressivism tend to be irritated by such statements, because from their point of view, schools and teaching are dominated by the same old dull approaches to education that they have been trying to change for more than a century. And they believe that our schools' ineffectiveness is due precisely to the influence of these traditionalist ideas. Progressivism, in their view, has never been implemented. In the 1960s, Paul Goodman, echoing many before him and echoed since by many others, argued that as soon as attempts are made to apply progressivist ideas in schools, the ideas become "entirely perverted" (1964, 43); their radical nature first is watered down and then sinks into the persisting stale routines of the traditional classroom.

In this book I will show incidentally that both of these claims— that progressivist ideas have become central to educational thinking and that they have never been implemented on a significant scale—are largely true.

What ideas make up progressivism? The central belief—the most fundamental tenet—of progressivism is that to educate children effectively it is vital to attend to children's nature, and particularly to their modes of learning and stages of development, and to accommodate educational practice to what we can discover about these. That this belief is shared almost universally among educators today supports Cremin's observation about how widely progressivism's tenets have become the conventional wisdom of American education, and Western education generally. But it is precisely this belief that I will show is mistaken.

My argument will be unfamiliar, I think. I shall not be arguing against progressivism on the basis of the usual alternatives of "liberal" or "traditional" theories of education or because it is not adequately attuned to preparing students for jobs. My critique will be unfamiliar also, I suspect, because it will be coming from someone who has considerable sympathy with progressivist ideals.

Progressivism has historically involved a belief in attending to the nature of the child, and consequently its research arm (so to speak) has involved studies to expose that nature more precisely. Because the mind is prominent in education, psychology became the consistent scientific handmaiden of progressivism. The psychologist exposes the nature of students' learning or development and the practitioner then must make teaching methods and curricula accord with what science has exposed. ("Education, therefore, must begin with a psychological insight into the child's capacities. . . . It must be controlled at every point by reference to these same considerations. . . . The law for presenting and treating [educational] material is the law implicit within the child's own nature"; Dewey 1964, 430, 435.)

One or another form of progressivism has been promoted and tried in the schools of North America since the beginning of mass schooling in the late nineteenth century. Progressivist practices have usually been promoted on the grounds that if only teachers will attend to the new knowledge gained by research about learning or development and follow what that research implies for teaching or curricula, an educational revolution will occur. In each new generation, progressivist educators have first to explain what was wrong with their predecessors' attempts to implement the ideas—because the promised revolution consistently fails to occur—and then to explain why their new approach will do the job.

So we may see the attraction the work of the Swiss psychologist Jean Piaget (1896–1980) has had for progressivists. Piaget claimed to expose in a new and fuller way the nature of children's intellectual development, and from his work progressivist educators sought to learn how to apply those insights to educational practice. Or we may see the attraction of the cognitive science research that Howard Gardner uses to support what he has described as his "sympathy with the vision generally termed 'progressive'" (1991, 189). The problems with past attempts to implement progressivist ideas are, he thinks, reparable by drawing on "recent advances in our understanding of individual learning" (246).

My task, then, is to expose a flaw in what seem to me the most widely held beliefs among educators today. Although the ideas that I think are false are foundational to progressivism, they seem also to be held by many who might even consider themselves critics of progressivism—which is where Cremin's observation about the movement's tenets having become the conventional wisdom of American education comes in.

My subtitle includes some of the main figures whose work has shaped the modern forms of progressivism and modern conceptions of education. Of the three I mention, the least well known today is Herbert Spencer (1820–1903), whose crucial role in the formation of progressivism and whose influence on modern schooling seem to me much underestimated, for reasons I describe in Chapter 1. This may seem an oddly balanced work, in which Spencer receives the lion's share of attention and John Dewey (1859–1952), for example, is represented as drawing significantly on Spencer's work. Perhaps it might seem a little offensive to identify what is usually thought of as a quintessentially American movement as derived significantly from the work of another dead white European male. Causality in ideas is, of course, difficult to trace with any security. Spencer's is certainly just one of many voices promoting not dissimilar ideas during those years on both sides of the Atlantic. Even so, although you may take the centrality of Spencer in my account as merely a kind of rhetorical stand-in for others, those constant reprintings of his book strongly suggest that it was his words that were most read. Spencer allied Jean-Jacques Rousseau's somewhat romantic view of educating with the authority of science, showing how child-centeredness and science together could provide the engine that would modernize and transform education. Also, not entirely coincidentally, this emphasis on Spencer is a kind of backhanded homage on the centenary of his death in 1902.

But this is not a work of history. I do consider some historical figures, but only because it is sometimes easier to disinter the ideas that have been loaded with layers of complexity over the years by looking at their earlier appearance and then seeing how they have gradually transmuted into today's presuppositions. It is a way of trying to make strange what is so familiar that we find it hard to think about. My topic is current education and how the persistence of powerful progressivist ideas continues to undermine our attempts to make schooling more effective.

"The world is largely ruled by ideas, true and false," observed the American historian Charles A. Beard (1932, ix). He went on to quote a "British wit" to the effect that "the power which a concept wields over human life is nicely proportioned to the degree of error in it" (ix). We needn't give in to such cynicism, of course, but the witty point pricks because it sometimes seems true. The power that Spencer's ideas have wielded over educational thinking is a sharp example of just this point.

In Chapter 1, I outline some of the basic ideas of progressivism, showing their early expressions in the work of Herbert Spencer. I also consider the strange case of Spencer's immense influence and almost vanished reputation. In Chapters 2 through 4, I look at progressivist ideas about learning, development, and the curriculum. In each case I begin with Spencer's formulations—which will, I suspect, surprise many readers, as they may have come to take such ideas as obviously true and might even believe them to have been originally Dewey's ideas. I show how such figures as Dewey and Piaget elaborated these ideas, how they have found their way into current practice, and how they have been wrong from their beginning and haven't become any less wrong for a century's reiteration. In Chapter 5, I argue that much modern educational research is flawed by related presuppositions to those I identify in progressivism. Throughout, I indicate the direction we need to move in to get beyond the pervasive flaw.

When I mentioned to a colleague the proposed title of this book—"Getting it wrong from the beginning"—he said cheerfully, "Ah, an autobiographical work!" I have indeed been trying for some years to work out a way of describing an alternative view of how we might better educate children in the modern world. This book may be seen as a companion to two others, the slim center between two larger chunks of text. The first of this trilogy of sorts is *The Educated Mind: How Cognitive Tools Shape Our Understanding* (University of Chicago Press, 1997), and the third, forthcoming from Yale University Press, is skulking under some aggressive, and provisional, title such as "How to Educate People." All three explore related issues, and there are necessarily small overlaps in each. The books form part of a project to provide a fundamental critique of current educational theories and practice and to outline an alternative that might move us toward more effective schooling in modern societies. I want to make the case here that most of the beliefs most of the people hold about education today are wrong in fairly fundamental ways. As my colleague declared, maybe I'm getting it wrong. But that's for you to decide.

chapter 1

. . . .

THE STRANGE CASE

. . . .

OF HERBERT SPENCER

. . . .

I will describe the essential ideas of progressivism through the work of the least well known of my subtitle's stars, Herbert Spencer. Although John Dewey's educational ideas are widely known today, in many regards, they are built on the bases laid by Spencer, though Dewey harnessed them to quite different social and political agendas. The third figure I consider, Jean Piaget, wrote two books about education, but neither advances progressivist theory much; Piaget's contribution lies rather in his developmental ideas. Spencer's formulations are important because nearly everyone involved in establishing the new state schools in the late nineteenth century read them. The influence of ideas is rarely easy to establish, but it would be very odd to deny the author of these ideas an important role in shaping modern schooling and forming progressivist educational theory.

Apart from the huge number of publications of his various works, and their translations into many languages, Spencer was offered (and refused, where possible) honors from learned societies in the United States, England, Italy, Denmark, Belgium, Greece, Austria, and Russia. Some thinkers held what may seem now wholly extravagant valuations of his work. The novelist and critic Arnold Bennett, who read Spencer's *First Principles* on his honeymoon during the winter of 1906–1907, wrote: "If any book can be called the greatest in the world, I suppose this can. . . . it is surely the greatest achievement of any human mind. . . . as a philosopher, he is supreme in the history of human intelligence" (1933, 192). Bennett, of course, was hardly an expert critic of philosophy, as he admitted, and maybe the conditions of the reading affected his delight in the text, but nonscholarly readers widely shared his view. Even someone as unlikely as Matthew Arnold wrote that he often read Spencer as a kind of bracing for his mind (Honan 1981). The American educator F. A. Barnard wrote, "We have in Herbert Spencer not only the profoundest thinker of all time, but the most capacious and most powerful intellect of all time. Aristotle and his master were no more beyond the pygmies who preceded them than he is beyond Aristotle" (Hofstadter 1955, 31). The *Atlantic Monthly* in 1864 declared: "Mr. Spencer has already established principles which, however compelled for a time to compromise with prejudices and vested interests, will become the recognized basis for an improved society" (776).

Spencer's name is so rarely mentioned in educational writings today that it is easy to forget how avidly his book was read and reread by pretty well everyone involved in making the new state schools. This was especially the case in the United States. The influential clergyman and abolitionist Henry Ward Beecher wrote to Spencer in 1866 explaining that the "conditions of American society have made your writings far more fruitful and quickening here than in Europe" (Duncan 1908, 128). I am sure that many of the ideas I shall lay out here will be familiar, though perhaps readers will not associate them with Spencer: most tend to be credited to Dewey or taken as implications of Piaget's theories; or they are assumed to be products of recent notions like "constructivism" or even thought to have emerged from modern "grass-roots" practice. And of course, not all the ideas originate with Spencer—Locke and

Rousseau, to name two hardly forgotten figures, can also stake claims as originators. But Spencer is particularly interesting because his formulations were so influential at the crucial period when American public schools, and those of many Western countries, were being formed. And he wrapped these principles in the prestige of science, claiming them not as another set of philosophical speculations, such as those from the Swiss thinker Johann Heinrich Pestalozzi (1746–1827) or the German educators Johann Friedrich Herbart (1776–1841) and Friedrich Wilhelm August Froebel (1782–1852), but as scientific hypotheses.

. . . .

SPENCER'S EDUCATIONAL IDEAS

A context for Spencer's work includes two dramatic ideas that had created much intellectual ferment by the time his writings were becoming widely known. The first was articulated by the Scottish scientist Sir Charles Lyell (1797–1875). As a young man Lyell studied law, but he later developed a consuming interest in geology. Between 1830 and 1833 he published his *Principles of Geology,* in which he argued that all the available physical evidence supported the view that the earth was not created, as was widely held, in 4004 B.C. This date had been calculated more than a century earlier by Archbishop James Ussher (1581–1656), a renowned scholar and apparently a man of such charm and sweetness of character that his devotion to the royalist cause in England's civil war did not prevent him from being treated favorably by Oliver Cromwell or from being buried in Westminster Abbey. To arrive at this date, Ussher had totted up the years of the events in the Bible, counting backward carefully to the exact year of the creation.

Lyell argued instead that not only did a study of geology show evidence of gradual changes in the earth over immense spans of time but the forces that had brought about those changes were continuing to operate in the present. In place of an instantly created world, which had remained stable at least since the major catastrophes mentioned in the Bible, Lyell proposed a long-established world that was in a constant state of much more gradual change.

One could now retain one's faith in a 4004 B.C. creation if one believed that God had made the world with marks of eons of past changes and the bones of extinct animals already in it. Yet that sophistication, with its image of a playful or mysterious God sprinkling the created earth with clues to forms of life that had never existed, was not an idea that attracted wide adherence. Instead, in the nineteenth century combatants clashed for and against the new scientific view that conflicted with the claims of the Bible, if read literally.

Into this growing conflict came the vastly more disturbing second idea, the theory of evolution as propounded by Charles Darwin (1809–1882). There had for a long time before Darwin been theories of evolution; indeed Spencer himself had been promoting evolutionary ideas for many years before Darwin published *On the Origin of Species* in 1859. In his 1852 essay "The Development Hypothesis," Spencer had in fact used the word *evolution* and had propounded elaborate arguments about how it accounted for changes in history and society.

By the 1850s, then, many people accepted that some of the most widely held past beliefs about the world and about humankind's place in it were radically mistaken. For this receptive audience, Spencer published *Education: Intellectual, Moral, and Physical* in 1860. Here he argued that education, too, had been radically mistaken in the past. Education, he wrote, had been most often conducted by forcing irrelevant information into the minds of reluctant children by methods that were patently barbarous; instead, he proposed, we should draw on new scientific principles to make the process efficient as well as pleasant for the child. In the past, education had dealt with subjects that held their place in the curriculum by dint of tradition and the affectations to an ornamental culture of a leisured class; instead, he argued, we should make the curriculum of direct relevance and utility to the lives our students would actually lead. In the past, schooling was centered on the knowledge written in texts or authorized by teachers, whereas instead the child's own developing needs and expanding activities should be central to the curriculum and to teachers' efforts.

Spencer aimed to show how learning and development, and the daily activities of the classroom, were parts of the same laws that shaped the stars above and the earth below. Those laws shaped the evolution of human beings from simple organisms long before, and those same laws shaped the development of each child from the earliest moments in life to adulthood. In essence, Spencer argued that the whole cosmos was subject to natural laws and that these laws were accessible to scientific scrutiny.

The greatest and most fundamental of these laws is that we live in a dramatic universe that is subject to constant change and that this change follows an invariable development from the homogeneous to the heterogeneous or, as he sometimes put it, from the simple to the complex. We see this law operating in the earth's development from a largely homogeneous mass of molten material to such heterogeneity as cheap tin trays, cabbages, kings, imagined talking middle-class rabbits, and computer keyboards—to name a random few.

We can see the same laws operating in the cosmos at large, in the evolution of species, in the development of societies in history, and in the changes from the child's to the adult's mind. By observing how the cosmic principle of "simple to complex" plays itself out with regard to human psychology and its development through life, we can devise a new approach to education. This is what Spencer offered.

Beginning with the natural process of the child's development rather than with the knowledge one wants the child to learn, Spencer argued, creates a recognition that children are naturally inquiring, constructing, and active beings. So, the developing powers of children provide the basis for his educational philosophy.

Education, he believed, is concerned with the whole person, not just the intellectual part. We should be concerned primarily not to produce scholars in the old sense but rather with what a person most needs to know to be able to perform his or her duties in life most adequately. Spencer's curriculum, then, would no longer follow fashions of culturally prestigious subjects, such as Latin and Greek and details of European political history: "The births, deaths, and marriages of kings, and other like trivialities, are committed to memory, not because of any direct benefits that can possibly result from knowing them: but because society considers them a part of a good education—because the absence of such knowledge may bring the contempt of others. . . . Men dress their children's minds as they do their bodies, in the prevailing fashion" (1928, 2).

If we grant that there are observable regularities in children's development, then, Spencer pointed out, "it follows inevitably that education cannot be rightly guided without knowledge of these laws" (1928, 23). He felt that these laws were largely ignored in the educational practices of his time, and that, if only they were adhered to, the whole process of education could be made more efficient, effective, and pleasurable to the child and teacher. He emphasized how easily the child learns about "the objects and processes of the household, the streets, and the fields" (24) and argued that the educator should observe such effortless learning and explore how it could be replicated by sensible teaching.

Spencer underlined the centrality for successful learning of direct experience. We must recognize, and act on the recognition, that "the words contained in books can be rightly interpreted into ideas, only in proportion to the antecedent experience of things" (1928, 24). Spencer made a central principle of his pedagogy that children's understanding can expand only from things of which they have direct experience. Words in books about things of which they have no experience can be learned only in an arid sense. We can teach children to repeat back what is learned as might a parrot, but they may understand the meaning of the rote-learned words no better than would the parrot.

Traditional education, as Spencer put it, is primarily concerned with making "the pupil a mere passive recipient of other's ideas, and not in the least leading him to be an active inquirer or self-instructor" (1928, 25). By becoming such inquirers or self-instructors, children become active in making sense of their experience, just as they so effectively do in the home, street, and field.

"The rise of an appetite for any kind of information," Spencer argued, "implies that the unfolding mind has become fit to assimilate it, and needs it for the purposes of growth" (1928, 51). As we feed the body with the best and most appropriate foods at different stages of life so that it grows to its fullest potential, then so with the mind, we must provide the best food to further its fullest growth. We must constantly, as Spencer said, conform to the natural process of mental evolution. We develop in a certain sequence, and we require a certain kind of knowledge at each stage, "and it is for us to ascertain this sequence and supply this knowledge" (53).

Spencer laid out seven principles for intellectual education. The first is that "we should proceed from the simple to the complex." This, as he acknowledged, is a principle that has always been accepted in some degree. But Spencer elaborated a new sense in which it should be understood: "The mind develops. Like all things that develop it progresses from the homogeneous to the heterogeneous" (1928, 58). We must, then, recognize the gradual development of the mind and build our teaching and curricula so that they conform with and support that developmental process.

The second principle is that the "development of the mind, as all other development, is an advance from the indefinite to the definite" (1928, 59). Spencer believed that from original chaos order gradually emerged—an idea he carried over to the child's mind in his belief that children's cognition is initially indefinite, chaotic, and vague and gradually becomes more definite, ordered, and clear.

Spencer's third principle is that "our lessons ought to start from the concrete and end in the abstract" (1928, 60). This he considered crucial for all teaching, especially in the early years. He argued that abstract ideas are accessible and meaningful only in the later years of schooling, and even then he pointed out that introduction of new material should begin with concrete aspects of it from the student's experience and then move gradually toward abstractions. Elementary school lessons should deal always with the practical and the concrete, with children's everyday experience, which they understand by dint of their own explorations and active involvement: "In the child we see absorption in special facts. Generalities even of a low order are scarcely recognized, and there is no recognition of high generalities" (1966a, 354).

Fourth, the "education of the child must accord both in mode and arrangement with the education of mankind, considered historically" (1928, 60). Spencer believed that the child's experience was like that of our distant ancestors faced by the phenomena of the world around them and trying to comprehend them. Over the ages of active struggle with the material features of their lives, of speculation and experiment, human beings have gradually reached our current understanding. The mind of the young child similarly faces the puzzling phenomena of the world, and children follow a similar route by similar procedures in coming to a modern understanding. They recapitulate, to use Spencer's term, in a few years a process that has taken humankind millennia. Education may, then, learn from the process of cultural history how best to help the child's mind navigate the process of intellectual development.

Fifth, "in each branch of instruction we should proceed from the empirical to the rational" (1928, 61). We cannot organize knowledge meaningfully until we have first made it our own and understood it in our own way. "Every study, therefore, should have a purely experimental introduction" (62). So science begins with experiments in the everyday world around the child, geography begins with the immediate environment the child lives in, history begins with the events that impinge on the child's life, and so on. It is the practical, meaningful world of the everyday life of the child, in which can be found the originating material for our explorations out toward complex, organized knowledge.

The sixth principle is that "in education the process of self-development should be encouraged to the uttermost. Children should be led to make their own investigations, and to draw their own inferences. They should be *told* as little as possible, and induced to *discover* as much as possible" (1928, 62). This principle was to be a foundation stone of the new pedagogy. The teacher was not to be the most active members of the classroom. The teacher must not spend time *telling* students what they are to learn, as though telling were sufficient for learning; that simply makes children, in Spencer's words, "mere passive recipients of our instruction" (63). In the new educational scheme the teacher will be the facilitator of the child's active learning. As Spencer pointedly put it: "The need for perpetual telling results from our stupidity not from the child's. . . . Having by our methods induced helplessness, we make helplessness a reason for our methods" (63).

The seventh and final principle he posed as a question: "Does [learning] create a pleasurable excitement in the pupils?" (1928, 63). He continued: "Even when, as considered theoretically, the proposed course seems the best, yet if it produces no interest, or less interest than some other course, we should relinquish it; for a child's intellectual instincts are more trustworthy than our reasonings" (63).

The plan for education, then, is, as Spencer put it, "to guide the intellect to the appropriate food" (1928, 68). But the teacher must be ever aware that the child's instinctive tastes are the ultimate determiners of what is appropriate food for them; it is children's questions, their interests, and their constructive, inquiring intelligence that are the sole adequate engine of educational progress.

"Progress," of course, captures something essential about Spencer's educational beliefs. No wonder that the educational movement to incorporate his principles most fully was called "progressivism" in the United States. Spencer's book came along with a set of further ideas that gave those who took them to heart a great feeling of optimism. Teachers imbued with Spencer's ideas might have felt that they brought progressive methods to their schools against a hopeless weight of traditional teaching and thinking about education. But a further principle that Spencer derived from his general principle of homogeneity to heterogeneity gave these teachers hope. In his book *Social Statics*, of 1851, he argued that civilization is not rigidly marked off from the laws of nature but "is a part of nature; all of a piece with the development of the embryo or the unfolding of a flower" (1851, 65). There is, he believed, "a law underlying the whole organic creation," and the product of this law is, to quote again Spencer's central doctrine, that "progress is not an accident, not a thing within human control, but a beneficent necessity" (65).

So progressive teachers could be of good cheer as they introduced the new ideas and methods into their practice. They could see themselves as transforming their schools in the years to come, and through them, they would transform society in a progressive direction, under the guidance of beneficent necessity. And although, again, this idea might not be wholly original to Spencer—the marquis de Condorcet in 1795, awaiting execution during the French Revolution, argued that progress was inevitable and the perfectibility of the human race a mere matter of time, even if too long for him—the Englishman claimed to have established it as a scientific principle, not simply a philosophical speculation.

. . . .

SPENCER'S RISE AND FALL

If Spencer is so central to the construction of the schools of today, and has consequently influenced the education of nearly everyone in America, how is it that his name is almost forgotten, even within educational studies?

Herbert Spencer's name is perhaps known in a vague way by many professors of education, but most teachers have never heard of him. If he is mentioned in textbooks, it is usually in a casual footnote or in a reference to his extreme answer to his still disturbing question, "What knowledge is of most worth?" Even those I have mentioned as influenced by him—Dewey, James, Parker, Hall, Thorndike—are parsimonious with acknowledgments to Spencer, and his name appears in their writings most commonly when they are refuting one or another of his prodigal ideas. How could someone virtually no one today reads be the source of ideas nearly everyone in education accepts without question?

This section is something of an interlude in that I use it to account for Spencer's obscurity, despite his influence. It is not *merely* an interlude, because accounting for Spencer's obscurity begins, somewhat obliquely, a critique of his progressivist ideas.

In his introduction to Spencer's *Essays on Education, Etc.* (of which the first part was made up of the book we have been considering above), published in 1911, Charles W. Eliot, president of Harvard, noted that "the ideas on education which he put forward more than fifty years ago have penetrated educational practice very slowly—particularly in England; but they are now coming to prevail in most civilized countries, and they will prevail more and more" (1928, viii). (It's not entirely clear from the syntax of that sentence whether Eliot excludes England from the "civilized countries.") He added: "Many schools, both public and private, have now adopted—in most cases unconsciously—many of Spencer's detailed suggestions" (xiii). That "unconsciously" is worth emphasizing—already, at the beginning of the twentieth century, Spencer's ideas were becoming dissociated from his name.

In her autobiography, *My Apprenticeship*, the writer on sociology and economics Beatrice Webb (1858–1943) describes her early enchantment with Spencer's ideas, the ferment of intellectual excitement that he created, and then her disenchantment: "My case, I think, is typical of the rise and fall of Herbert Spencer's influence over the men and women of my own generation" (1971, 61). What brought about so precipitous a fall that even those American educators who enthusiastically drew on his ideas were reluctant to acknowledge him as their source?

Spencer's voluminous writings bring to mind what was one of the most famous Victorian cartoons to appear in the British humor magazine *Punch*. The cartoon, composed by George du Maurier, was known as "the curate's egg" and appeared under the title "True Humility." At two ends of a long table sit a weedy, nervous young curate and a portly, domineering bishop. They are having boiled eggs for breakfast, and the wavy lines rising from the curate's egg indicate that it is rotten. The bishop says, " I'm afraid you've got a bad Egg, Mr. Jones." The diffident curate replies, "Oh no, my Lord, I assure you! Parts of it are excellent!"

Spencer's work, as the century wore on, came to be seen as

curate's egg-ish. Parts of it may have been excellent, but the bad parts were found so unpalatable that his great influence dissipated rapidly. I mention six reasons for this decline here, focusing particularly on those connected with educators' reluctance to acknowledge him as their source. (See also Kazamias 1966, on which some of the following gratefully draws.)

First, those who enthusiastically adopted Spencer's educational ideas for the new state schools faced the embarrassment that Spencer argued resolutely against any provision of education by the state, especially for the lower classes. He believed that state education would, among other defects, create undesirable uniformity and stifle original thought. Many proponents of universal education by the state believed that it would have immense social benefits. Spencer argued that such optimism was drastically misplaced (see Samuel and Elliot 1917). To people like John Dewey, who were concerned deliberately to expand public schooling, using the state's control of schooling to reconstruct society through educational reform, Spencer's views were, to say the least, inconvenient. This was especially true because the general principles from which he derived the progressive educational ideas the reformers liked were also the principles on which he founded his opposition to public schooling. His version of social evolution led him to believe that the only chance the weak, poor, and unintelligent had of progressing was by living in the face of oppressive odds and passing on to their children, by some Lamarckian evolutionary mechanism, the coping skills they learned. Alternatively, they should be discouraged from breeding. Education and other social welfare programs undermined both processes and so, in his view, only fostered incompetents and so slowed down the beneficent progress nature has in store for us.

Second, the ideas commonly labeled "social Darwinism" might be better called "social Spencerism," as many have suggested. "The survival of the fittest" was originally Spencer's term, even though Darwin did later use it in a limited way. Spencer extended the idea of the survival of the fittest from natural selection to pretty well everything in sight. When he applied it to society and to economic systems, he argued for what British prime minister Edward Heath called "the unacceptable face of capitalism"—that is, the exploitation of the poor, weak, and defenseless by the rich and powerful for the latter's private profit. This aspect of Spencer's supposedly scientific writings helped account for his great popularity with one segment of American society. William Sumner (1840–1910), president of Yale University, enthusiastically used these ideas of Spencer's to argue for the freedom of capital from state regulation. Association with a ruthless program of exploitation and suppression of working people, and with a program of unstinting support for a power elite, hardly endeared Spencer to socialists like John Dewey or to any of those who advocated using the new schools to further democratic ideals. The biologist Thomas Huxley, fairly or not, summed up Spencer's social ideas as "reasoned savagery" (1951, 181).

Spencer's horror of socialism and associated ideas was such that he refused to read Rousseau's book on education, *Emile,* despite some of his own views on wealth distribution and despite people's pointing out similarities in some of their proposals. When Beatrice Potter announced her intention to marry the socialist Sydney Webb, Spencer ditheringly retracted his request that she be his literary executor, pleading that his association with someone who was associated with a socialist might shock people.

Third, even at the level of curriculum development, where Spencer's focus on the whole life of the child and on learning things of practical value was warmly embraced, his own application of the principles produced an exclusively science-based curriculum, even in primary school. This reflected Spencer's peculiar education by his father and uncle, but it seemed simply eccentric to those who were planning to prepare the young for all aspects of life in an expanding American society.

Fourth, some of Spencer's fame grew from his having devised theories about evolution before Darwin published his arguments and evidence. As mentioned, "evolution" was Spencer's coinage. Darwin at first wrote of "descent with modifications" or "natural selection," neither of which had the snappy neatness of Spencer's preferred term, which became the one generally accepted, even by Darwin. The problem was that Spencer never really understood Darwin's idea of natural selection. He seems to have seen Darwin's theory as simply one particular mechanism—a clever one, undoubtedly—whereby evolution proceeded and as one small addition to his own vastly more comprehensive philosophical theory of evolution.

Yet Spencer's scientific understanding never advanced beyond a rather crude Lamarckian view. Jean-Baptiste de Lamarck (1744–1829) had proposed in his *Philosophie zoologique* of 1809 a groundbreaking theory of evolution; he argued that changes occurred in species when acquired characteristics were passed on to subsequent generations. So if a species were moved to a new environment in which, say, a tail no longer served a useful purpose, the tail would disappear over generations and other features that were more used would be enlarged or expanded in some way. The classic example given of this inheritance of acquired characteristics was of giraffes' necks stretching over generations the better to reach the high vegetation of tall bushes and small trees.

Lamarck's general idea of species change has become widely accepted, as has Darwin's explanation of how it occurs. By the end of the nineteenth century, when Darwin's theory had become more widely understood, those most committed to evolution considered Spencer outdated, eccentric, and ignorant. So one of evolution's most outspoken champions became a decided embarrassment. William James, in his *Principles of Psychology* of 1890, took issue with Spencer about evolution, pointing out that he simply misunderstood it.

Fifth, on the scientific side, matters became even worse for Spencer. In 1853, the ideas about energy expenditure of the German physicist Hermann von Helmholtz (1821–1894) were translated into English. His formulation of the second law of thermodynamics had terrible implications for the principle from which Spencer had spun most of his general theories, including his main educational ideas. Spencer had absorbed Karl Ernst von Baer's (1792–1876) notion of "the law underlying the whole organic creation" (1851, 65)—that we are parts of an immense process that moves inexorably from the homogeneous to the heterogeneous. The second law of thermodynamics claimed the opposite: that energy is being endlessly dissipated in work, light, and heat, so the cosmos is moving inexorably to an homogeneously dark, silent, dead universe.

Helmholtz's law led to some panic in midcentury, as physicists tried to calculate how long the sun could continue to expel its heat and light before burning out; estimates ranged from a bothersome twenty-five years to ten million years.

What, then, happens to Spencer's beneficent nature and its guarantee of progress? Later in the century, as Beatrice Webb touchingly chronicled, Spencer was a deeply depressed and disappointed man. She wrote: "In answer to my inquiry [about why Spencer found the new physics so disquieting] my friend Bertrand Russell suggests the following explanation: 'I don't know whether he was ever made to realize the implications of the second law of thermodynamics; if so, he may well be upset. The law says that everything tends to uniformity and a dead level, diminishing (not increasing) heterogeneity'" (Webb 1971, 109n).

We know he was made to realize the implications by the Irish physicist John Tyndall (1820–1893), and Spencer's shaken reaction is on record; he was indeed deeply disturbed, and remained so more or less until his death.

More modern astrophysics, of course, makes the whole matter much more complicated, and Helmholtz's law perhaps applicable only in limited ways. Yet although Spencer's principle might be saved in some interpretations, it is hardly on the basis of his understanding of cosmology.

Sixth, another embarrassment for the educational reformers was Spencer's belief in recapitulation. This was his fourth guiding principle for educators: "the education of the child must accord both in mode and arrangement with the education of mankind, considered historically" (1928, 60). Spencer also believed that this principle had been shown to operate in biology, drawing again on Baer. He followed the mid-nineteenth-century conviction that the developing human fetus went through—recapitulated—all the stages of development of our species, from a simple-celled creature, through gilled fishlike ancestors, and so on, to the present. Like so much of the primitive science Spencer picked up, this, too, was shown to be false.

But among those Americans who influenced the new schools there was clearly ambivalence about this idea. One enthusiastic believer in educational recapitulation was G. Stanley Hall. He believed, with Spencer, that a child's learning should follow the process whereby the different forms of knowledge had been built up during cultural history. John Dewey was also clearly attracted to recapitulation early in his career, noting that there "is a sort of natural recurrence of the child mind to the typical activities of primitive people" (Gould 1977, 154). Even later, Dewey occasionally used recapitulationist arguments to support his curriculum proposals, for example, "It is pertinent to note that in the history of the race the sciences grew gradually out from useful social occupations" (1966, 220–221). But at the same time, he explicitly rejected recapitulation with the claim that it "tends to make the . . . present a more or less futile imitation of the past" (75). He saw recapitulation as incompatible with the educational task to "emancipate the young from the need of dwelling in an outgrown past" (73). In reaching such a position Dewey echoed Edward L. Thorndike's more forthright rejection of recapitulation: "Heaven knows that Dame Nature herself in ontogeny [the development of each individual] abbreviates and skips and distorts the order of the appearance of organs and functions, and for the best of reasons. We ought to make an effort, as she does, to omit the useless and antiquated and get to the best and most useful as soon as possible. We ought to change what is to what ought to be, as far as we can" (1913–1914, 1:105).

The additional embarrassment about Spencer's recapitulationism was its casual and brutal racism. His theories helped those whose interests lay in viewing other races as inferior "savages," comparing such adult "savages" with modern children: "During early years every civilized man passes through that phase of character exhibited by the barbarous race from which he is descended. As the child's features—flat nose, forward-opening nostrils, large lips, wide-apart eyes, absent frontal sinus, etc.—resemble for a time those of the savage, so, too, do his instincts. Hence the tendencies to cruelty, to thieving, to lying, so general among children" (1928, 108). Spencer used such absurd observations to justify "superior" people's right to govern "inferior" people and, of course, to decide who was inferior and who superior. With American schools' need to prepare huge numbers of immigrant children for the new society, recapitulation was clearly an unattractive idea, and the support evinced for it further repelled most educators.

By the first decades of the twentieth century, then, if you were an educator attracted by Spencer's educational principles, you would not likely be keen to declare yourself a follower of Spencer. The accompanying baggage would be too burdensome. Although many were still ready to acknowledge Spencer in the 1880s, it became increasingly convenient to cite homegrown American authorities who expressed his ideas without reference to him.

The trajectory that Beatrice Webb describes Spencer's reputation as following can be traced vividly in the experience of the psychologist and philosopher William James (1842–1910). On first reading Spencer in his late teens and early twenties, James was excited and awe-stricken at the range and daring of the English writer's ideas. It came as a disturbing blow when James heard the mathematician and logician Charles S. Peirce (1839–1914) attack Spencer in the early 1870s (James 1978, 116). After using Spencer's two-volume *Principles of Psychology* in his Harvard course on physiological psychology and examining more closely some of Spencer's general ideas and methods of supporting them, James became increasingly critical. By the late 1870s, James had become exasperated by much of Spencer's methodology and by many of his most general conclusions. He wrote facetiously but also with real vehemence to James Putnam about Spencer and his disciples: "Down with the hell-spawn of 'em! Of all the incoherent, rotten, quackish humbugs & pseudo-philosophasters which the womb of all-inventive time has excreted he is the most infamous and 'abgeschmackt' —but even he is better than his followers" (Skrupskelis and Berkeley 1995, 563–564).

In the end, James published five critiques of Spencer's work (see Lempert 1997—from which much of the above information about James is taken). He endorsed those critics who "likened [Spencer] to a kind of philosophical saw-mill, delivering, year in and out, with unvarying rectilinear precision, paragraph after paragraph, chapter after chapter, book after book, as similar one to another as if they were so many wooden planks" (James 1978, 97).

How can someone deride Spencer's ideas and yet find his educational principles attractive? Well, there is the curate's view of the rotten egg—parts of it may be considered excellent. James had concluded that Spencer's most fundamental ideas were worthless, but he acknowledged that in some of his observations, and clearly his educational ideas are included here, Spencer was admirable, clever, and ingenious (see Perry 1935, 1:374).

• •

BEATRICE WEBB'S AND SOME OTHERS' VIEWS OF SPENCER

Before going on, though, it might be interesting to view Spencer as educator and scholar, as seen through the eyes of someone who worked closely with him. Spencer was a friend of Beatrice Webb's parents, Richard and Laurentia. He greatly admired Richard Potter, despite his "complete indifference to the working of the philosopher's intellect" (Webb 1971, 48). Evenings were commonly spent, witnessed by young Beatrice, in which Spencer would engage in some argument or discussion with Laurentia Potter, and the two would energetically pursue their "unsettleable controversies" (Spencer 1904, 1:311) until long after the weary but good-natured husband retired to bed. Webb described Spencer as she recalled him from her early years:

> Finely sculptured head, prematurely bald, long stiff upper lip and powerful chin, obstinately compressed mouth, small sparkling grey eyes, set close together, with a prominent Roman nose—altogether a remarkable headpiece dominating a tall, spare, well-articulated figure, tapering off into diminutive and well-formed hands and feet. Always clad in primly neat but quaintly unconventional garments, there was distinction, even a certain elegance, in the philosopher's punctilious manners and precise and lucid speech. [1971, 48–49]

As an educator, he "always appeared in the guise of a liberator" (Webb 1971, 49). Whenever he observed the Potter children's lessons with the governess he railed against her manner of teaching—complaining to the Potters about "stupid persons who taught irrelevant facts in an unintelligible way" (49). And here is the reply Webb recorded: "'You can go out this morning, my dears, with Mr. Spencer,' said the governess to her pupils, after listening with pursed up lips to one of the philosopher's breakfast tirades against discipline, 'and mind you follow his teaching and do exactly what you have a mind to'" (49). In the governess's sarcastic response we hear the beginnings of what will be a more than century-long conflict between the progressivist demand for freedom to explore against the traditionalist sense of the importance of discipline.

Still, Webb writes that as the years went by, she and Spencer were on the whole firm friends, and his work as her tutor certainly cannot be said to have had anything but remarkable effects—though the effects seem to have resulted less from Spencer's methods in practice than from Webb's own remarkable mind in constant interaction with Spencer's fertile intellectual activity. As she wrote: "Speaking for myself, I was never interested in these collections of animate and inanimate things, even when looked at through his microscope or pulled to pieces by teasers. What fascinated me, long before I began to study his writings, was watching him collect illustrations for his theories" (1971, 50).

Her concern was with his method of building his theories:

But by the time I became his companion these "First Principles" had ceased to be hypotheses; they had become a highly developed dogmatic creed with regard to the evolution of life. What remained to be done was to prove by innumerable illustrations how these principles or "laws" explained the whole of the processes of nature, from the formation of a crystal to the working of the party system within a democratic state. Herbert Spencer was, in fact, engaged in the art of casuistry, and it was in this art that for a time I became his apprentice, or was it his accomplice? Partly in order to gain his approbation and partly out of sheer curiosity about the working of his mind, I started out to discover, and where observation failed, to invent, illustrations of such scraps of theory as I understood. What I learned from this game with his intellect was not, it is needless to remark, how to observe—for he was the most gullible of mortals and never scrutinized the accuracy of my tales—but whether the sample facts I brought to him came within the "law" he wished to illustrate. [1971, 50–51]

Spencer's method of constructing vast theoretical structures on suspect foundations is well captured in one of the more celebrated and brutal put-downs in recent intellectual history, an exchange reported by the English mathematician Karl Pearson in 1909 (Abrams 1968, vii). In the presence of Thomas Huxley and a few others, Spencer said: "You fellows would little think that I wrote a tragedy when I was young." Huxley immediately said: "I know what it was about." Spencer was surprised at this and said it was impossible that Huxley could know, for he had never mentioned it to anyone before. But Huxley insisted, and Spencer challenged him to describe it. Huxley replied: "It was the history of a beautiful induction killed by a nasty little fact."

Beatrice's sister Kate, who became Lady Courtney after marriage, recalled that "Mr. Spencer certainly had a keener desire than most men to get other people to adopt and carry out his views, even on quite trifling subjects: such as how to light a fire, or revive it when it was low, the hanging of pictures, the colours in a carpet or the flowers on a dinner table, the proper shape of an ink-stand, and a thousand other matters; and he allowed what he thought our unreasonable way of doing these things, even when they had nothing to do with himself, to unduly disturb his peace" (Duncan 1908, 73). Spencer, a lifelong bachelor, had a keen desire to get everyone to adopt and carry out his views on child-rearing, with no little success. The note of irritation in Lady Courtney's comments is echoed in many accounts of Spencer's character and reflects her sister's view that Spencer possessed not a "ray of humility" (Webb 1971, 107). (When he had begun his *Principles of Psychology,* he wrote to his father that the book would "ultimately stand beside Newton's *Principia*"; Kennedy 1978, 47.)

Spencer seems to have been irked by Darwin's huge success. Because Spencer's evolutionary ideas preceded Darwin's, at least in time of publication, he couldn't really see why Darwin got so much credit when the idea of "natural selection" was just one mechanism, Spencer thought, operating in a process whose most general principle he himself had elucidated at length. Toward the end of his life, when revising the major books he had written in the 1850s and 1860s, Spencer punctiliously preserved his claim to an earlier and more general theory than Darwin's. He refused to change his Lamarckian beliefs, keeping intact such claims as: "While the modified bodily structure produced by new habits of life is bequeathed to future generations, the modified nervous tendencies produced by such habits of life are also bequeathed" (1897, 422). He typically dealt with Darwin in footnotes, such as the one attached to the above passage: "Had Mr. Darwin's *Origin of Species,* been published before I wrote this paragraph, I should, no doubt, have so qualified my words to recognize 'selection,' natural or artificial, as a factor. . . . But . . . while holding survival of the fittest to be always a cooperating cause, I believe that in cases like these it is not the chief cause" (423).

Yet despite his fatal sloppiness and in spite of Beatrice Webb's conclusion that thirty or forty years of intimacy with Spencer's unique intellect served her well as a warning no less than as a model, she wrote movingly of the philosopher's deep concern whenever she was sick as a child, of his suggested remedies for any ailment, of his constant and patient support of her first struggles to write, of his arranging for the immediate publication of her first essay in social investigation, and of the example of his "heroic disregard of material prosperity and physical discomfort" in concentrated intellectual work that he saw as in the public good (1971, 53). One must also be ready to forgive much to someone who was the only survivor of nine children and wonder about the pressures he must have faced as a boy. So, if Spencer is in some sense the villain of my book, he is a villain who exhibited in some of his personal relationships great kindness and in his life's work heroic virtues.

With Spencer, what we have is a set of ideas that by the end of the nineteenth century were either shown to be wrong or were outmoded, eccentric, and confused. To invoke his name in support of particular educational practices, then, was to raise too many hackles and to inspire opposition. And yet, although nearly all of Spencer's scientific and social ideas are now considered museum pieces, the principles for education that he derived from them have become the taken-for-granted folk wisdom of education today and profoundly shape current practice. I will go on now to argue that we should put Spencer's educational principles in the museum, too, and show their fundamental flaw that persists within progressivism.

Curiously, this might contribute in a small way, in educational thinking, to the result Beatrice Webb foretold in her final meeting with Spencer. She visited him when he was close to death in Brighton, south of London. He was agitated about his reputation and influence, feeling that he had become of no consequence in the intellectual world that had once lionized him. She soothed him by saying, "What you have thought and taught has become part of our mental atmosphere, Mr. Spencer. And like the atmosphere we are not aware of it. When you cease to be our atmosphere, then we shall again become aware of you as a personality" (1971, 59).

After Spencer's death, William James, in a lecture at the Lowell Institute in Boston in 1906, asked why a thinker of such obvious insufficiencies remained so popular that "half of England wants to bury him in Westminster Abbey" (1988, 329). In spite of Spencer's "preference for cheap makeshifts in argument" and vague ideas, James concluded that the general support for Spencer resided in the fact that "we feel his heart to be in the right place" (329).

An attempt was indeed made to have the atheist Spencer memorialized in Westminster Abbey shortly after his death, even though during his life he had turned down all honors offered to him and asked for the simplest cremation and burial of his ashes. The letters concerning the issue "reveal that the details of Spencer's work were largely forgotten and that [the] correspondents were divided on whether Spencer had been simply a controversialist or had done something worthwhile. Even those (the majority) who believed the latter were unable to articulate exactly what was worthwhile in Spencer's work" (Gay 1998, 41–42).

In *Facts and Comments*, his final book of essays, published in 1902, which Spencer introduced with the cheerless observation that "the volume herewith issued I can say with certainty will be my last" (82), he wrote a sentiment that may well seem obvious to any atheist but that only a deeply disappointed person would articulate: "With his last breath it becomes to each the same thing as though he had never lived" (289). In his last conversations with Beatrice Webb, he concluded that "of literary distinction, as of so many other things which men pursue, it may be truly said, that the game is not worth the candle. . . . the satisfaction which final recognition gives proves to be relatively trivial" (Webb 1971, 29).

chapter 2

. . . .

LEARNING

. . . .

ACCORDING TO

. . . .

NATURE'S PLAN

. . . .

Like nearly everyone involved with education, Spencer observed that in "the household, the streets and the fields" (1928, 24) children are able to learn all kinds of things effortlessly, with eager pleasure, yet these same children often have great difficulty learning quite elementary things in formal educational settings. How to explain this puzzle? Why should children who learn to talk fluently later find it so hard to learn to read and write fluently or learn a second language as easily as the first? Why should children who rapidly become so easily initiated into the norms and values of one culture find it so difficult to accommodate to those of another culture later in life? Why should children who find it easy to learn the sometimes complex rules of games find it hard to grasp simple mathematics?

Spencer believed that his studies of evolution, biology, and psychology had given him the answer. He confidently claimed "that the evolution of intelligence in a child . . . conforms to laws; and it follows inevitably that education cannot be rightly guided without knowledge of these laws" (1928, 23). When children fail to learn in schools, the fault usually lies in the methods of instruction or in the failure of the curriculum to conform with the laws whereby children's intelligence and learning work.

The answer Spencer proposed was to devise methods of instruction, learning environments, and a curriculum that did conform with the underlying laws of children's learning and development. Once methods and curricula more hospitable to children's natural modes of learning were in place, their desire for knowledge would be released, and a revolution in learning would occur.

The progressive movement in particular, but many others, too, have been convinced of this idea, and in the twentieth century immense amounts of time, energy, ingenuity, and money were expended on trying to make learning in schools match children's spontaneous learning in household, street, and field. The holy grail of progressivism—to let the metaphors run free—has been to discover methods of school instruction derived from and modeled on children's effortless learning and so bring about the revolution promised by Spencer and by progressivists throughout the twentieth century. In spite of all this ingenuity, effort, and money, the revolution hasn't shown much sign of occurring.

I'm not in the business of arguing that significant improvements in general education are impossible, but I am committed to showing why Spencer's progressivist prescription for education's problem hasn't worked and can't work.

So what is the error? Well, it's more like two related errors—a bad one and a worse one. Let's take the bad one first. Consider philosophical psychologist Jerry Fodor's model of the human mind as composed of a set of fast and "stupid" input systems, each of which has its own dedicated processes and is focused on specific stimuli in the environment. The input system concerned with language learning, for example, attends to linguistic data and ignores other data, and it works so "stupidly" that we can't *not* learn a language, unless there is damage to the relevant parts of the brain.

These fast input systems then reformulate their data to make them accessible to the general-purpose central processor. In Fodor's model, then, we have fast input systems and a slower, more deliberative central processor. I use Fodor's terms here as a shorthand way of indicating the bad error, even though there may be reasons to question Fodor's model, as Annette Karmiloff-Smith (1992), among others, has argued. But his model is useful simply to indicate why one might begin to worry about the "common-sense" objective of making children's learning in schools conform with their effortless learning in households, streets, and fields. What is being required, in Fodor's terms, is to make the central processor work like an input system. It won't and can't. The century and more of attempts to make school learning more like children's early effortless learning have been misdirected. Well, that's to oversimplify the argument, and the following pages will involve us in some complexifying.

The worse error I want to expose, in Spencer's writings and today, is connected with the common belief that children's minds have some preferred natural kind of learning and that if we can isolate and understand it we can then make the educational process more efficient and effective. I will show why we should abandon this belief and look elsewhere for the key to enhancing the efficiency and effectiveness of children's learning.

. . . .

NATURE'S PARADIGM OF HUMAN LEARNING

The year after Spencer's death in 1902, William James published in the *New York Evening Post* an essay—"Herbert Spencer Dead"—that tried to give as favorable an interpretation of the Englishman's work as James could bring himself to write (see Lempert 1997). Among his judgments of the massive Spencer oeuvre, James concluded that *The Principles of Biology, The Principles of Sociology,* and *The Principles of Psychology* "must soon become obsolete books" (1978, 100). *The Principles of Biology* is rarely cited now, except as a horrible example of what can go wrong if one builds complex theoretical edifices on factually flawed foundations. *The Principles of Sociology* does rather better, in texts about the origins of the discipline; Spencer's doctrines are considered obsolete, but he gets points for originality and for trying to bring social processes under some law-like survey. (Mind you, some commentators argue that "modern British sociology was built, more than anything else, as a defense against Spencer"; Abrams 1968, 67.)

The Principles of Psychology seems, like a big stone rippling a pond, to have faded completely away over time. Reading the two volumes of *The Principles of Psychology* today can be a tad dispiriting. Apart from the ubiquitous racism, the organization of all facts, and "facts," around the dogma that all the processes of the changing world follow a path from a state of relatively indefinite, incoherent homogeneity to a state of relatively definite, coherent heterogeneity is like watching a fairly clumsy conjuror constantly repeating the same trick with far too much worn-out equipment. But Spencer claimed that he was exposing, among other things, the fundamental nature of human learning.

My aim here is not to hammer Spencer for failing to have incorporated into his theorizing all the findings of late twentieth-century neurophysiology and cognitive science. Rather, I wish to show that the principles so many educators still find attractive are as problematic as their source in his psychology.

Nature's plan, as Spencer outlines it, is to deliver a baby with just a few basic reflexes but with a power of learning that "lies latent in the brain of the infant" (1897, 1:471), created and furnished by the long process of evolution. The simplest actions of the infant impinge on the environment, and from the reaction of the environment, the child begins to construct an understanding of the world. Here, briefly, is Spencer's way of putting it:

> The organism is placed amid immeasurable relations of all orders. It begins by imperfectly adjusting its actions to a few of the simplest of these. To adjust its actions more exactly to those few simplest, is one form of advance. To adjust its actions to a greater variety of these simplest, is another form of advance. To adjust its actions to successive grades of the more complicated, is yet another form of advance. [1897, 1:418]

Gradually we adjust our inchoate and incoherent senses to the ordered environment, and as our perceptions become sharper and clearer and take in more of the environment, they lead eventually to ideas and adult understanding. Our early experiences lead to concepts that progress by differentiation and integration (1897, 1:624–628). Our internal sense of the world gradually mirrors ever more precisely the world outside, following "the law which Intelligence fulfills more and more the further it advances" (418): "Only by supposing such a law to exist can we explain the facts, that relations which are absolute in the environment are absolute in us, that relations which are probable in the environment are probable in us, that relations which are fortuitous in the environment are fortuitous in us" (417).

Spencer does not try to delineate how the operation of the basic law of learning he identifies in these simplest interactions between infant and environment reaches full adult understanding: "Everyone must . . . admit that the steps by which these simplest inferences of the infant pass into these inferences of high complexity drawn in adult life, are so gradual that it is impossible to mark the successive steps" (1897, 1:461). It is clear to Spencer, though, that the same fundamental law applies equally from the earliest and simplest learning to the most mature and complex.

Some of Spencer's ideas are, of course, at least as old as Aristotle and can be traced through John Locke, David Hume, and others. The basic idea from which these modern beliefs derive seems to be Aristotle's notion that every living thing has a natural form and that each organism's growth is determined by an innate need to reach the fullest realization of that form. Once the mind is viewed as a kind of organism, it, too, is conceived in these terms. (Aristotle's spells are hard to break. In a careless moment he wrote that flies have four legs. Despite the easy evidence of anyone's eyes, his magisterial authority ensured that this "fact" was repeated in natural history texts for more than a thousand years.)

One of Spencer's original themes was the manner and degree of environmental responsibility for the conception of the world built up in the child's mind. The result of Spencer's study of psychology is an odd sense of the mind passively accepting the impress of the environment's regularities while requiring an active organism to attract as many impressions as possible.

Armed with this law, what we can do, Spencer suggested, is observe the child's most characteristic forms of learning in the natural environment when no deliberate teaching is taking place. The trick then would simply be to "systematize the natural process" and adopt the methods of teaching that nature has been perpetually thrusting upon us, "if we but had the wit to see it, and the humility to adopt it" (1996b, 84).

From his conclusions about the mind and the learning process, Spencer made these now-familiar proposals for shaping what happens in educational institutions to be more like what happens in natural learning in the child's everyday environment: the child must be active not passive; learning occurs best through play in the early years; new knowledge must be connected with what children already know and will thus initially be concerned with the local, the concrete, and the simple; learning should be pleasurable and not forced; and so on. By the end of this book, I will hope to have persuaded you that each of these common principles should be mistrusted.

(That they remained commonly believed seems too obvious to need much exposition. Eyes closed, I reached out and took a book from my "early childhood" shelf and spent a few minutes flipping through the pages; a pity it is an older one, but I didn't feel I should go back, having used the eyes-closed rule. One finds such observations as "children have a natural inclination to explore and manipulate," Hildebrand 1981, 37; "The children become personally and actively involved in their own education. They are helped to find concrete ways of relating new knowledge to what they already know," 80; "play is very valuable," 38, with sixteen particular values of play then listed; "Children are more likely to understand and remember information that they discover themselves," 80; "learning takes place following sensory stimulation from people, things, and activity in the environment," 172; and so on, including pervasive promotion of "activity.")

Spencer's *Principles of Psychology* is spotted with examples of his conclusions applied to pedagogy, in the form of appealing brief scenarios of a kind still familiar in education texts. Reflections on logic lead him to invite his readers to suppose "I am giving a child a lesson in Mathematics, carried on after that concrete method which teachers, were they wise, would habitually adopt as an initiation" (1888, 2:91). He sits with the child playing marbles. The child has fifty marbles and Spencer demonstrates that one can make squares of four marbles on each side and see that these squares have sixteen marbles in them. With fifty marbles one can make three such squares and have two marbles left over. Or one can make squares with five marbles on each side; two of such squares will use up all fifty marbles. One can classify the marbles and form sets based on those that are chipped or have striped designs, and so on. Thus Spencer begins the child's understanding of mathematics while playing with familiar and simple concrete objects, showing how "sensible experience" carries the child's mind "to the numerical truths" (91). (Mind you, if I'd been the child playing marbles, I'm not sure I'd have found this adult's game more engaging than the ones I had been playing before he came along and interfered.)

Of course, the use of play as a paradigmatic form of natural learning is hardly new. Plato observed that one shouldn't "use force in training the children in the studies, but rather play. In that way you can also better discern what each is naturally directed towards" (*Republic* 537a). Plato also described this as a procedure practiced long ago by the Egyptians.

The ideal example of an educational practice that violated all of Spencer's principles but was still commonly used was "the vicious system of rote learning" (1966b, 30). Rote learning has remained for progressive educators the epitome of the unnatural, forced, and meaningless: "To repeat the words correctly was everything; to understand their meaning nothing," and it was a method that could operate only by "threats and bribes" (61).

The related epitome of bad educational practice was to teach rules first and examples later, as in "that intensely stupid custom, the teaching of grammar to children" (Spencer 1928, 50). "The particulars first and then the generalization, is the new method," Spencer declared, in the 1850s (1966b, 61). The student should also *experience* the particulars, not simply be *told* them.

The educational principles he had outlined would, Spencer believed, prepare students to become skeptical of the daily press and other fashionable rubbish and ensure an end to producing the useless, ornamentally educated minds that were prevented from seeing what nature was thrusting on their attention. Like Karl Marx in 1848 announcing the specter of communism stalking Europe, before most people had even heard of it, Spencer announced the imminent universal success of the new principles of learning:

> The forcing-system has been, by many given up. . . . The once universal practice of learning by rote, is daily falling more into discredit. All modern authorities condemn the old mechanical way of teaching the alphabet. The multiplication table is now frequently taught experimentally. In the acquirement of languages, the grammar-school plan is being superceded by plans based on the spontaneous process followed by the child in gaining its mother tongue. [1966b, 60–61]

Spencer might be saying the same today—as many do. Why, he and his modern followers wonder, cannot educators attend to the principles of learning exemplified so straightforwardly when children are active and at play in their everyday environment? Why, instead, do teachers become caught up forcing an artificial curriculum into children's minds using outdated methods, making the learning painful and inefficient for the child and the teaching frustrating and inefficient for the adult?

Part of Spencer's success in stimulating a revolution in educational theory if not in practice was due to his rhetorical strategies. Apart from his own conviction, and his presenting learning as some kind of binary moral choice between the traditional, passive, forced, and vicious and the progressive, active, effortless, and pleasurable, he constantly interspersed his arguments with attractive and plausible images of the new methods at work. In contrast with an image of frustrated and unhappy children toiling indoors over dull textbooks, consider this typical example of Spencer's descriptions of his proposed methods in practice: "Every botanist who has had children with him in the woods and lanes must have noticed how eagerly they joined in his pursuits, how keenly they searched out plants for him, how intently they watched while he examined them, how they overwhelmed him with questions" (1966b, 86).

Who could be against methods that promised such scenes of eager learning? But consider, as something of an astringent drawn from reality, Beatrice Webb's account of just such an outing with Spencer. When Beatrice and her siblings were released from their governess's traditional classes and given over to Spencer's educative care, she exuberantly describes how "the philosopher found himself presently in a neighboring beech-wood pinned down in a leaf-filled hollow by little demons, all legs, arms, grins and dancing eyes, whilst the older and more discrete tormentors pelted him with decaying beech leaves" (1971, 49). This might indeed have been of more value in some ways to the children than lessons with the governess, but Webb's account of Spencer's pedagogy leaves one to wonder: "We agreed [as children] with his denunciation of the 'current curriculum,' history, foreign languages, music and drawing, and his preference for 'science'—a term which meant, in practice, scouring the countryside in his company for fossils, flowers and water-beasties which, alive, mutilated or dead found their way into hastily improvised aquariums, cabinets and scrap-books—all alike discarded when his visit was over" (50).

Obviously it is unfair to use this example as typical of what happens when Spencer's principles are put into practice. But the gap between the predictions of what will result from engaging children's "natural" learning and the result from trying to do so in practice has been consistently very wide. To committed progressivists, it is also something of a puzzle, and each generation that recommends much the same principles has to give a new explanation why their predecessors failed to produce the promised results in the past.

Spencer took many of his principles from Johann Heinrich Pestalozzi. Spencer acknowledged that the Pestalozzian system held great promise, but "we hear of children not at all interested in its lessons—disgusted with them rather" (1928, 55). How to explain this failure? Even with "the choicest tools, an unskilled artisan will botch his work" (56). That is, it was the teacher's fault—a reason we have heard again and again for the gap between what ought to happen and what does.

The other common excuse is that the previous generation got "nature" wrong—they misunderstood the nature of learning or the nature of development, but an ever-advancing science will, or has, exposed more precisely or clearly or correctly the *real* nature of learning or process of development—which is then used to justify the same progressivist scheme.

* *

NATURAL LEARNING IN THE TWENTIETH CENTURY

The beliefs I am criticizing are not simply the confusions of Herbert Spencer, and so merely of historical interest. The same ideas recur time and again through the century and a half since he wrote. The confusions that surrounded the setting up of mass public schooling are still with us, in much the same form, and we are still bombarded with the same "solutions." With regard to the beliefs about learning outlined above, it seems harder to find people who don't accept them than to show examples of their persistence and influence through the twentieth century into current practice. (Indeed, my diligent and intelligent research assistant found so many examples that they dwarfed my manuscript.) So I won't take up a lot of space piling quotation on quotation. I'll first cite influential educational thinkers and curriculum documents that have shaped schooling, then show how these beliefs undergird some prominent programs and texts used in schools today.

Rousseau was, of course, an unacknowledged source of Spencer's general idea that we have natural forms of learning that should determine how we teach, or facilitate the learning of children. But Spencer gave the idea a distinctive form, imbued it with the authority of science, and bequeathed to twentieth-century educational thinkers his principles of natural learning in contrast with artificial and forced learning. The distinction between the natural and progressive and the forced and traditional was prominent in the educational landscape throughout the twentieth century.

The educator's task, for Dewey as for Spencer, was to work out how to replicate in schools the natural learning one sees in children's play and basic orientation in households, streets, and fields. The child in preschool years is engaged in "personal and vital" learning, and the "educator who receives the child at the end of this period has to find ways of doing consciously and deliberately what 'nature' accomplishes in the earlier years" (Dewey 1963, 74). When it comes to devising methods of instruction, Spencer's principle that we must "systematize the natural process" (1966b, 84) is glossed by Dewey as: "The law for presenting and treating material is the law implicit within the child's own nature" (1964, 435).

Well, it would be idle to keep quoting Dewey to show how the educational principles for which his work is revered are largely echoes of Spencer's principles. That doesn't mean, of course, that Dewey merely echoes Spencer, though there is a significant amount of echoing. Dewey had his own agenda, which went in directions quite different from Spencer's.

In *Democracy and Education,* Dewey mentions Spencer only once. Unable completely to ignore Spencer, who had already and famously made arguments for the importance of developing scientific understanding in students, Dewey remarks: "Herbert Spencer, inquiring what knowledge is of most worth, concluded that from all points of view scientific knowledge is most valuable. But his argument unconsciously assumed that scientific knowledge could be communicated in ready-made form. Passing over the methods by which the subject matter of ordinary activities is transmuted into scientific form, it ignored the method by which alone science is science" (1966, 221). As a distancing move, this might serve Dewey's purpose, but as an account of Spencer's beliefs, it is close to libelous. It was Spencer, after all, who required that all learning be based on children's "antecedent experience of things" (1928, 24) and who recommended sitting down to play marbles to lay a concrete, active, experiential base for later mathematical principles. The nineteenth-century advocate of discovery methods should not have been so treated by the twentieth-century advocate.

Early in the twentieth century the same basic points are repeated again and again. Another influential voice, W. H. Kilpatrick, tells us, in *Education for a Changing Civilization*, that "a new and more reliable psychology" (we will hear *that* theme again) directs us to "demands that the school become more truly a place of actual experiencing, for only in and from such experiencing can the child get the inherent close-to-life kind of education formerly given by his home and community" (1926, 96). He wanted "the school to furnish experiencing typical of the best experiencing to be found outside the school" (103). Echoing Spencer's dislike of rote learning even of the multiplication table—which Spencer wanted learned "experimentally"—Kilpatrick writes: "As to the multiplication table, my pupils will not see any such table until they themselves perhaps *live* the making of it. They will, however, *live* numbers as these enter into their other living" (318).

I have trawled through the century finding constant repetitions of these same beliefs about learning. I can't see that I need to drag you through this echo chamber. What is slightly odd is that the constant re-echoes of these ideas tend to be presented as the novel, radical, insights of the echoers. No doubt the 1960s and early 1970s movement for radical educational reform will still be a partially living echo in current educational writing. In this movement, the traditional schools and their methods of teaching were represented as the main agents that "stifle children's natural capacity to learn" (Gross and Gross 1969, 13). Paul Goodman complained of the increasing unnatural schooling visited on children and announced the new program of the reformers to do away with the artificiality of schooling, by deschooling if necessary, so that children's natural learning could be released: "We must drastically cut back formal schooling because the present extended tutelage is against nature and arrests growth" (1964, 86). From different perspectives in the 1980s we have arguments by David Elkind (1981) and Neil Postman (1982) that claim that the currently dominant forms of education contravene the child's natural development and learning, and they propose, again, new ways of making these institutions conform better with nature's preferences. And through to the end of the twentieth century, we find books continuing to claim that new research, now prominently under the label "cognitive science," has more adequately exposed how children learn and from this research new programs of education are articulated. "Science now offers new conceptions of the learning process and the development of competent performance. Recent research provides a deep understanding of complex reasoning and performance on problem-solving tasks and how skill and understanding in key subjects are acquired" (Bransford et al. 1999, xi). From such findings new programs that better conform with children's modes of learning are shaped. Apart from some of the terminology, these new programs look very much like Spencer's old program.

Let me, then, turn from the writing of educationalists, with the endless complaints about rote learning and the endless assertions that a more reliable psychology has or will delivered principles that show us how to make learning natural and efficient, and look briefly at one of the more prominent current programs that is putting into practice what its proponents describe as a new paradigm. It is hard to catch a fashionable movement in education before the caravan moves on, and I have chosen Whole Language perhaps a tad late, for it has begun to come into disrepute in increasing segments of the educational world, but I am confident that it will have a successor soon, promoting the same ideas and practices.

"Never have I witnessed anything like the rapid spread of this recent movement away from mechanistically driven and towards child-centered approaches to teaching reading," writes P. David Pearson (1993, 504). Whole Language and Authentic Literacy approaches, Pearson claims, dominate current practice and how teachers are instructed in education courses concerned with reading. (It is, of course, hard to assess how accurate such claims are. Certainly they are largely true in my experience of institutions, but even there, most professors of education are sensible people and are rarely committed wholly to a single approach; they instruct about alternative methods as well.) From Spencer's point of view, failures to learn adequate literacy would be ascribed to the teacher imposing artificial methods, ignoring the child's natural mode of learning, and failing to recognize the proper role of play and pleasure that must be part of the active learning process.

I could here reproduce lengthy quotations from dozens of texts promoting "whole language" and "authentic literacy" that are very largely extended echoes of Spencer. I'll just take a few exemplary texts. The whole language classroom, we are told, is designed to conform to how children naturally learn; it is like "homes where children are allowed and encouraged to be learners from the day they are born" (Peetoom 1988, 246). The learning in such classrooms is active—the children construct their own understanding and do not passively internalize the ready-made, artificial lessons of traditional textbooks. "The key to whole teaching and learning is the active involvement and enjoyment of children as they play with, manipulate and construct language through exposure to fun, enjoyable, rich, and meaningful literature" (Polette 1990, 19). Anything that looks like rote learning is anathema; the classroom is not a place where "the knowledge of one generation is passed to the next" (Peetoom 1988, 245).

"In the old paradigm, teachers are merely transmitters of someone else's knowledge" (Peetoom 1988, 247), whereas in the new paradigm children are viewed as accomplished learners when they arrive at school and "the teacher should intrude only minimally into this process of discovery" (Altwerger 1994, 40). Spencer's belief that the teacher should merely facilitate the child's active discovery is a central tenet of whole language: "Teaching is not 'teaching' at all. It is an act of guiding and appreciating" (Martin 1990, 3), whose whole purpose is to free the child "from fears and drudgeries all too often associated with language learning" (10).

Frequent reference is made to the ideal learning of early childhood and how new research has begun to focus on "how children themselves learn, in their homes and classrooms" (Peetoom 1988, 246). This research supports the principles very familiar to us by now and has provided the basis for designing the whole language classroom as "a timely extension and enrichment of the home" (246).

"Whole language is a paradigm shift" (Peetoom 1988, 246). (It is hard not to view this claim somewhat wryly from Spencer's 1850s perspective.) The "new paradigm" perpetuates Spencer's binary distinction between natural, "whole," "real," "authentic," learning in contrast with artificial, synthetic, traditional forms, and insists that the choice between the two has a moral tinge as well as the former being scientifically supported by the latest research (see Moorman et al. 1994).

As a final note, whole language does seem so like the "Quincy system" of Francis W. Parker (1831–1902) that talk of new paradigms is a bit of a stretch. Parker had studied in Germany and was influenced by Herbart, Froebel, and Pestalozzi. But he also acknowledged and clearly exemplified his debt to Herbert Spencer. The system of reading instruction he introduced in Quincy, Massachusetts, in the late 1870s threw out traditional grammar books and taught reading as far as possible the way children learned to speak. Instruction was designed to support the child's learning according to nature's plan.

In repeating much the same set of principles, beginning with Spencer's articulation of them, and then echoes that persist to the present I wish to stress that they are not simply some old forgotten principles of learning but are still very commonly proposed and supported ideas. Although Spencer's language might be a little antique, commitment to the basic pedagogical principles of learning he articulated has changed hardly at all in the intervening century and a half within progressivism.

. . . .

WHAT IS WRONG WITH PROGRESSIVIST PRINCIPLES OF LEARNING?

"For a species that spends so much of its time thinking, we don't have much of a handle on the subject," Derek Bickerton has observed bemusedly (1995, 57). We might say the same about "learning."

To describe what is wrong with progressivist ideas about learning I must show, a bit tediously I'm afraid, why we should be suspicious of the belief that the mind has a preferred mode of learning that is evident in young children's effortless mastery of a range of knowledge and skills. I will then show why claims that children should begin with the concrete and simple are misleading, why we should cease to believe that students should begin with what they know, why we should discard such principles as preferring active to passive learning, and why the long opposition to rote learning has been a disaster. Such criticisms of standard beliefs require the criticizer to come up with a viable alternative, so I will. I have already indicated that I consider the traditional-liberal education principles equally as problematic as the progressivist beliefs I am criticizing, so I won't be trotting out those stale and shopworn alternatives. Rather, I will sketch what seems to me a viable way of conceiving learning in educational institutions that overcomes the problems inherent in both progressivist and traditionalist practice.

In this chapter I am concerned mainly to deal with progressivism's more fundamental beliefs about learning and indicate an alternative. In the following Chapters 3 and 4, I similarly challenge basic progressivist beliefs about development and the curriculum.

The Mind as Undiscovered Country

Spencer's homogeneous to heterogeneous law requires that human beings start life outside the womb with virtually nothing in the way of mind and then gradually learn from the environment's tutelage the array of knowledge of the typical adult. In his scheme, we start from "low and vague beginnings" (1897, 1:627), when our thinking is "simple, vague, and incoherent" (617); this general condition is evident, he assures us, to anyone who has observed the "vacant stare of the infant" (617). Perhaps the most famous exposition of this notion is William James's description, in his *Principles of Psychology*, of infants perceiving only a booming, buzzing confusion. (If leaving behind vagueness and confusion is the prime criterion of intellectual development, I fear that I'm heading in the wrong direction; "booming, buzzing confusion" seems an increasingly good description of the state of my mind. Oddly, James wrote "blooming," but I have followed what has become the almost invariable misquotation, taking it as indicating what most people prefer the phrase to mean.)

No one familiar with research on infant cognition during the past quarter-century or so can take Spencer's views seriously. It is precisely the infants' intelligent staring at particular features of their environments that has provided a tool to investigate their early knowledge and learning. In Chapter 3, I detail some of the cognitive competencies of infants, the discovery of which has decisively undermined all those schemes based on babies' supposedly blank minds. What is particularly important here is that the accumulating evidence of infants' surprising range of knowledge and intellectual competence should not be seen as evidence of general cognitive abilities. That is, what infants can do, though surprising in light of millennia of theories that asserted the "blank slate" or empty condition of the mind at birth, is nevertheless limited and quite precise. Some of Piaget's experiments with hidden toys suggest how infants conceptualize the world quite differently from adults. As Howard Gardner puts it: "Try to get an infant to recognize faces upside down, or a toddler to speak a language which does not make phonemic distinctions or which requires that the child attends to every other word. You will soon discover the powerful, specific constraints on cognition in *Homo sapiens sapiens*" (1997, 26). Effortless ease in one kind of intellectual act goes together with incapacity in acts that can look very similar. That is, all learning is not alike. Some forms of learning are evolutionarily shaped to solve very precise and constrained problems, and consequently do not provide good models for general domain-unspecific learning.

My further purpose is to show that the process Spencer described, and on which he then based his central claims about methods of learning and teaching, is wrong. And I want to focus on its wrongness so as to raise problems for the methods of learning and teaching that form a centerpiece of progressivism and are largely taken for granted today.

So I want to emphasize the irregularities, the peculiarity, and the differentiations in forms of human learning. The mind we have inherited from our evolutionary history is not one whose accumulation of knowledge and understanding proceeds in some gradual, regular, spontaneous, and undifferentiated way. This should be easier to recognize now since it is generally accepted that our evolutionary history is also quite unlike the gradual process Spencer imagined. Rather, in the process of our evolution we have experienced "radical reengineering of the whole brain" (Deacon 1998, 45). Our brain is like the product of an ingenious *bricoleur,* a scavenging odd-job tinkerer, reshaping and reusing old parts for new purposes, adding bits, attaching new to old bits, gerrymandering a functional—occasionally inspired, occasionally clumsy—organ. As Merlin Donald puts it: "modern human cognitive architecture is highly differentiated and specialized. . . . the modern mind is like a mosaic structure of cognitive vestiges from earlier stages of human emergence" (1991, 2–3), and it has gone through "a series of radical evolutionary changes . . . rather than a continuous or unitary process" (Donald 1993, 737; see also Bickerton 1990, Lieberman 1984, and Plotkin 1988).

The most straightforward challenge to the belief that we have a single, undifferentiated learning process comes from theories such as Jerry Fodor examines, mentioned earlier. That the mind deploys some different modes for learning different things, particularly early in life, is an idea whose current prominence owes much to the work of Noam Chomsky. His argument that children's experience of language is too fragmented and sparse for them to build up the complexity of regular syntactic structures evident in the average three- or four-year-old has been influential in the crumbling of behaviorist beliefs about learning. One can also observe patterns in children's language-learning that make no sense if one assumes that their learning is shaped entirely by their environment. They make some mistakes—like saying, "I seed your feets"—that are a result of misapplying grammatical rules but are not learned from their environment since no adult says such things. And in learning certain forms of language, they virtually never make mistakes. For example, if one child has a single doll and another child has three dolls, and you say, "Give me a doll" or "Give me the doll," even three-year-olds will not be confused about whom you are addressing.

Chomsky argues that because classical theories cannot account for these features of language learning, they must be explained by something else. The best candidate for "something else," he and others have argued, is a part or parts of the brain "programmed" or genetically encoded for language learning. That is, we don't simply have some general learning ability that we use to master language and then turn it to learning algebra or phone numbers or faces or names or what hairstyle is fashionable. Language and faces seem to require very little effort. It is as though experience acts less as the whole source of such learning and more as a trigger with minimal information that kicks the program into action. Similarly, learning faces just isn't, notoriously, like learning names or phone numbers, even though the last two contain much less information than the first.

The power of our predisposition to learn language is evident in the cases of deaf children who have no signing parent. Such children invent visuomanual systems that display several of the features of natural languages (Goldin-Meadow and Feldman 1975). The relative specificity of language centers in the brain is indicated by results of localized brain damage in deaf adult signers. They can imitate the physical movements involved in a sign but have become incapable of using such signs for linguistic purposes (Poizner et al. 1987). Annette Karmiloff-Smith suggests that such findings support the theory that we possess a "domain-specific, innately guided process that can get language acquisition off the ground even in the absence of a model. . . . And when a linguistic model is available, young children are clearly attentive, not to some domain-general input, but to domain-specific information relevant to language" (1992, 38).

For many cognitive psychologists, the specialization of brain functions is no longer open to dispute. As Howard Gardner sums it up, "Recent research on early infancy provides the strongest clues to the inherent modularity of human cognition" (1997, 26). He goes on to make the point that "empirical evidence shows that the mind —human or pre-human—is distinguished *precisely* by the fact that it does not . . . harbor all-purpose rules or operations" (26). Gardner's own work (1983, 1993) on multiple intelligences is, of course, a vivid indicator of diversity in human learning.

Whether modularity is the best account of the evident differentiation in human forms of learning remains to be seen. (And it is worth attending to the arguments of those who see it as just a new form of phrenology; see Horgan 2001.) It would have been convenient to wait fifty years before writing this chapter so that greater definition of the neurophysiological evidence might be given. I am not convinced by the modular thesis, certainly in some of its versions (see Mithen 1996), and find Karmiloff-Smith's account in *Beyond Modularity* (1992) more attractive in some regards. The overall accumulation of evidence at present, however, at least establishes that human beings do not have a single mode of learning that is evident both in children's rapid mastery of knowledge in streets, fields, and homes and in their mastery of Latin irregular verbs and whose character has been captured in Spencer's principles.

So Spencer's nature, which has been urging sound methods of teaching on us, is obviously itself a capricious pedagogue. It puts immense investment into ensuring that we learn a language, track moving objects efficiently with our eyes, classify flora, and so on but seems to care hardly at all about our mastering irregular Latin verbs (unless we are Roman children long ago) or basic algebra.

So, the first flaw in progressivism exposed so far is the belief that human beings have a mode of learning whose paradigm form is evident in the way young children effortlessly learn language and other knowledge of the world in informal settings. If it is the case that we *do not* have such an undifferentiated mode of learning, then it follows that we *should not* assume that learning in school settings must be made to conform as closely as possible to this early effortless learning.

This argument, I realize, will not persuade convinced progressivists to reduce their commitment to progressivist ideas. After all, it isn't such basic psychological beliefs that they consider crucial. They will point out that more recent research, such as I have drawn on, is no less convincing to them as to me. The practices that engage active learners with meaningful material are, they will say, supported by modern research and modern psychological theories, and Spencer's nineteenth-century beliefs are beside the point. My point, however, is that those nineteenth-century theories were used to support a set of educational practices, and those practices have survived, despite what people may think is the state of psychological play. That is, the belief that we know enough about the mind and its development to continue to require active learning, begin with the concrete, avoid rote learning, and other practices is false. What little we know about the mind disrupts the beliefs that are still used in support of these methods. The second error—that we have a preferred form of learning that psychological research has exposed or will or can expose—I consider in the next section and more fundamentally in Chapter 5.

Psychology's influence on education has been so pervasive that we forget that topics like "learning" and "development," which may be investigated as different processes within psychology, are not so obviously distinguishable from an educational point of view. I mention this because the first set of issues I want to tackle below might equally well, or perhaps better, have come under the heading "development." I put them here because they are principles much referred to in discussing "learning" and because they are also fairly basic issues that are more easily discussed at the beginning of my attack on progressivist principles in practice. But I also indicate some of the developmental ideas of Spencer, Dewey, and Piaget that have supported them.

Simple to Complex, Concrete to Abstract, Known to Unknown: And Other Myths

A basic principle urged on educators is that we must make teaching and curricula "subservient to that spontaneous unfolding which all minds go through," in Spencer's words, or that methods in education are "ultimately reducible to the question of the order of development of the child's powers and interests" (Dewey 1964, 435), or teaching and curricula must be "subordinated to spontaneous and psychological development" (Piaget 1970, 716). We should have no difficulty agreeing with these claims if their authors could convince us that they could adequately describe the developmental process to which educators' actions need to be made subservient.

Perhaps, instead, being practical folk in the education business, we can examine some of the educational recommendations that follow from their principles. Let us take one of Spencer's central inferences from his homogeneous-to-heterogeneous generalization that remains, as far as I can see, almost universally believed by teachers and is constantly reiterated in textbooks—rather like the claim that flies have four legs. Spencer tells us that we should begin teaching young children with the "concrete"—as in his example of teaching arithmetic with marbles—and move in later years toward the abstract.

Is Peter Rabbit concrete or abstract? How about his relationship with the small birds who implored him to exert himself in order to escape from the gooseberry net in Mr. McGregor's garden? (I confess that I had to do some research with primary sources here.) Or how about the anxiety generated by the story of Hansel and Gretel in the forest? Concrete or abstract? Of course, the categories make little sense applied to such material, even if they are the kinds of stories most readily engaged by young children. Such categories might make *some* kind of sense if one focuses exclusively on learning basic scientific knowledge but hardly any sense at all if one focuses on the imaginative life of the child.

Why, if "concrete" and "abstract" are far from useful terms in discriminating features of children's thinking and learning, are they still constantly used in educational texts? They became, in significant part due to Spencer's influence, the terms people learned to use in thinking about children's thinking. They became concepts people thought *with,* and so they have become increasingly like preconceptions that people then don't think *about.* If we pause and step back and think about how adequate "concrete" and "abstract" are for classifying features of children's thinking and learning, we can, it seems to me, only be bewildered that they should have been so casually accepted for so long—not quite up there with four-legged flies, but close.

How can the characterization of young children as "concrete" thinkers survive the evidence of their ready grasp of symbols? Symbols are abstract, and are arbitrarily connected with what they symbolize. By age four, children who are exposed to symbols do not confuse writing, numbers, and drawings, for example. They have no apparent difficulty in grasping that symbols refer to things. Spencer's belief that the child must first learn by experience and experiment, not by rules, and that we must present knowledge "to the child in the concrete" (1966a, 70), never seems to have been challenged by his considering what kind of experience "and" or "but" represent or how they could be taught in the concrete. That children learn to deploy such terms in rule-governed ways, that they eagerly engage with characters and settings that were previously entirely unfamiliar, that their language and thought is suffused with abstractions, seems to me compelling evidence that this prime example of Spencer's main generalization about children's learning and cognitive development is wrong.

Even so, the belief that children are concrete and not abstract learners has had, and continues to have, an immense influence on children's education. I'll look at particular programs based on this strange belief in the next chapter and show how they impoverish the experience of schooling for many children.

One might take each of Spencer's principles and show their inadequacy. How can one hold as a general developmental principle that human learning progresses from the simple to the complex when we see nearly all children mastering language and complex social rules while most adults can't program a VCR? Obviously there are significant differences between what children typically know and can learn and what adults can know and learn. The question that is crucial for the educator, and very difficult to sort out, is just how to characterize these differences and characterize the process of development from one to the other. We need to face the fact that accepting general principles like simple to complex and concrete to abstract—and basing educational programs on them—is just not adequate. Those principles hide and falsify important features of the process. The source of these ideas was a false cosmology, transformed into a mistaken evolutionary theory, converted into a flawed psychology, and then inferred into those misleading educational principles.

Let us consider what has been perhaps one of the most persistent and powerfully influential of this set of principles; that one must start with what the student knows and then gradually expand knowledge from that base. Spencer's evolutionary beliefs led him to assert that children's early and simple experience had to form the basis for all future learning and that there must be a regular and orderly progression from what is already familiar to what is slightly less familiar—that expansion "by slow degrees to impressions most nearly allied." Nearly every teacher and professor of education I have encountered believes this principle. Most people assume it to be so obviously true that even to question it suggests a degree of nuttiness. (The principle is more commonly associated with the work of Johann Friedrich Herbart and with later Herbartian educational psychology. From that source as well as through the increasing influence of Pestalozzi, it became prominent in North America during the 1880s.)

Every educational textbook I have seen reinforces this belief: "If I had to reduce all of educational psychology to just one principle, I would say this: The most important single factor influencing learning is what the learner already knows. Ascertain this and teach him accordingly" (Ausubel 1968, 235). Apart from this slightly odd way of putting Spencer's principle, we should be wary of accepting it. You may think that I'm going to get myself into real trouble now, trying to argue against something that is obviously true. Well, if you think that it's true, here are four things for you to worry about:

First, if this is a fundamental principle of human learning, there is no way the process can begin.

Second, if novelty—that is, things unconnected with what is already known— is the problem for human learners, reducing the amount of the novelty doesn't solve the problem. And if we can manage some novelty, why can't we manage more?

The third objection is less directed at the principle than at how it has been invariably interpreted in education, and particularly in the construction of the elementary social studies curriculum (which

I look at in Chapter 3 as an example of a modern application of these ideas). It is assumed that what children know first and best is the details of their everyday social lives. That is, it is assumed that children's thinking is simple, concrete, and engaged with their local experience. But children also have imaginations and emotions, and these, too, connect with the world. Back to Peter Rabbit: If children's minds are supposed to be restricted to the everyday details of their social lives, why are they full of monsters, talking middle-class rabbits, and titanic emotions? I elsewhere (1997) have commented on the absurdity of explaining Peter Rabbit's appeal in terms of its "familiar family setting," when it involves a safe woodland and a dangerous cultivated garden, and death so close, and so on. Again, not only does the common interpretation of the principle seem to have this fatal flaw, but it embodies something close to contempt for children's intelligence.

Fourth, and this is the four-legged fly item, a few moments' reflection should make clear that no one's understanding of the world expanded and expands according to this principle of gradual content association.

Now, given the almost universal acceptance of this principle, and the fact that these four reasons may have little impact on most who believe it, I should add what seems to me the reason that such ideas survive so tenaciously. The principle survives because, like most knowledge claims in education, it is a mixture of analytic truth and empirical generalization. That is, at some level, the principle is true simply because people define its terms to mean something that can't be other than true. So it is understood to mean something like, you don't know whatever you don't know and if you learn something new, it has to fit in with what you can find comprehensible. If you don't speak Chinese and are told the solution to the three pagodas puzzle in Chinese, you will be unable to understand it. If you do speak Chinese, and know what pagodas are and understand the puzzle and other prerequisites, you will be able to understand the solution. At this level, the principle isn't very helpful. What would make it interesting are reliable empirical generalizations; that is, research showing conditions that constrain learning that are other than logical truths. We largely lack these in education because researchers commonly mix up analytic elements—things that are true by definition or by logic—with empirical components—things that could be otherwise but are discovered to be true as a result of experiments. By consistently mixing the two, we get claims that are assumed to be empirical generalizations resulting from research but whose generalizability relies heavily on the analytic component hidden in how the research is set up. I'll return to this in some detail in Chapter 5.

Active and Passive Learners

For progressivists, it is the artificiality and passivity of schooling tasks that is the problem. Learning ought to be "natural," tied in with the meanings of children's daily lives. They have the description of the problem right, but they have the diagnosis wrong in subtle ways. And so the prescriptions that follow the diagnosis are also wrong and fail to cure the problem.

My counterargument leads to questioning what is interpreted as "active" and "meaningful," for example. Who on earth could be against active, meaningful learning and in favor of passive, meaningless learning? What I want to show is that particular practices that engage children in active, meaningful learning do so not for the reasons progressivists give but for other reasons.

What Lawrence Cremin meant when he said that the analytic categories of progressivism had become the conventional wisdom of America education by the 1950s becomes evident when someone tries to criticize progressivists' acceptance of active, effortless, pleasurable learning. Those old progressivist assumptions trigger the further assumption that critics must be in favor of passive, forced, and labored learning. Yet those binary categories are as flawed as the beliefs from which they derive. The contrast has become so ingrained that it's hard to make the point that these just are not good categories to use in thinking about learning. The problem, again, is not that people think about these distinctions so much as they think about learning *with* them.

What does it mean to distinguish forms of learning as active and passive? Well, at one level we all know: they are terms used to distinguish lifeless, inert, boring practices from their opposite. But why "active" and "passive"? Is that child sitting and reading active or passive? Is the child imaginatively transported by a story the teacher is telling active or passive? A couple of days ago, I was in a third grade class and was asked—cunningly, by the student-teacher whose activities I was supposed to be observing—to read a story about owls as part of a unit the class was doing. Looking at the faces of the children as I read and showed them pictures in the book, I'd say that a number were clearly engaged, imaginatively entranced indeed, and some were clearly just not interested, busy fiddling with socks and so on. Which were active and which were passive? Well, the engaged ones, we might be tempted to say, were active and the others were passive.

As a casual way of distinguishing kinds of learning this may be fine. But look what tends to happen when such terms are used year after year, decade after decade. Instead of being understood as more or less vague indicators of a desirable feature of students' learning in a complex set of educational ideas such as John Dewey's, these terms become increasingly understood as indicating features of particular practices, often dissociated from, or misassociated with, the complex of ideas that initially gave them meaning. (Dewey, for example, notes that "mere activity does not constitute experience" [1966, 146] and that the "educative value of manual activities and laboratory exercises, as well as play, depends upon the extent in which they aid in bringing about a sensing of the *meaning* of what is going on" [246, emphasis in original].) The terms, though, become used to indicate features of practices that conform with the literal meanings of the words. These more literal meanings then become criteria for distinguishing good from bad practices. In good practices, children are "active," and so we are inclined to prefer practices in which children are patently engaged—and because we can see physical engagement better than intellectual, there is a tendency to move increasingly in that direction. So we get all that "hands-on" activity that, along with the strange belief that young children are "concrete" thinkers, has done so much to trivialize early education.

The Joy of Rote Learning

Consider Spencer's, Dewey's, and so many others' claim that rote learning is "vicious." This was paradigmatic of the traditional practices that progressivism has been trying to displace—in this case with some success. Students today, in my experience, are rarely asked to learn anything substantial by rote—or, to use an alternative term, by heart. Again, the trouble is not that we are thus able to displace stultifying practices but that the term becomes understood increasingly literally and separately from the complex of educational ideas that originally gave it meaning. Many young teachers I work with have been through educational programs that have persuaded them that it would be bad educational practice to make students learn chunks of text—poetry, prose, or anything—by heart.

Learning chunks of text is also neither effortless nor pleasurable, and certainly not "natural," and because we are to prefer these to their opposites, then such activities are also to be avoided. A result of this principle being taken literally and becoming one of the things people think *with* about education, is that students are deprived of developing those resources that come along with a wide and immediate access to some of the world's greatest poetry and prose. That they know where to go to find such poetry and prose perpetuates the absurdity of believing that this is the same as knowing something. Knowledge does not exist in books or in computer files. They contain only codes that require a living mind to bring them back to life as knowledge.

Knowledge exists only as a function of living tissue. Knowing where to find knowledge or poems or speeches is nothing like having that material as a part of one's living tissue. It affects how we think and feel, and education is about precisely improving these things. The emphasis that has led away from rote learning, and in this way eventually learning by heart, has been one that gradually and greatly impoverishes minds. This is how progressivism's flaw —in the name of the best impulse—has gradually undercut again and again the great purpose it was framed to serve.

. . . .

NATURAL LEARNERS OR TOOL INCORPORATORS?

Something quirky happened in our evolution to make us, uniquely, able to read and write, as you and I are both doing now—and able to enjoy in a mild and quirky way the humor and sadness of that ambiguous "now"; true for me on this wet and blustery spring morning, looking out at the tumbling apple blossom, and true for you I know not where and when. It is a strange contact. Terrence Deacon locates the quirk in our becoming a "symbolic species." Symbol use, though, seems just the tip of the iceberg of our oddity; it is a prominent oddity that pervades so much of what we do. Deacon says we are a species of idiots savants. We are savants in our preternatural intellectual development and in the symbol-use that has accompanied it, and we are idiots because we have become so caught up with symbol use that we cannot turn it off, even when it prevents us from acting sensibly and "naturally": "Like the character portrayed in *Rain Man,* who sees the world in terms of numbers of objects, we cannot help but see the world in symbolic categorical terms, dividing it up according to opposed features, and organizing our lives according to themes and narratives" (1997, 416).

Another aspect of our oddity is in our use of tools. We are, I suggest, idiots savants as tool users, too, and in ways that make human learning peculiar.

How has Spencer misled us here, or how has he epitomized the error we continue in? Spencer believed that science was exposing the nature of human learning. Learning was a property of the mind, and he conceived of the mind as a biological organ on the model of the body: "the mind like the body has a predetermined course of evolution" (1966b, 67). Psychology provided "the leading generalizations of the *science* of mental growth" (100). Or, as William James echoed Spencer's idea more succinctly: "Psychology is a science, and teaching is an art" (1901, 7). The reason we have been so ineffective in understanding the nature of human learning and in devising effective educational programs that foster mental growth is that beliefs like Spencer's continue to dominate psychological research on human learning. The largely unused key to understanding human learning, and the key to understanding what is wrong with educational proposals supposedly based on our natural forms of learning, is tied in with our peculiar relationship with tools.

I find it useful to begin reflecting on this peculiar relationship by considering Michael Polanyi's (1967) example of how we oddly extend our senses into the tools we use. Imagine being in a completely dark cave, feeling your way with a walking stick. What you feel is the impress of the head of the stick against your hand. But what you "feel" in the mind is the end of the stick against hard, flinty rock or soft, mushy moss or whatever. We have a peculiar way of incorporating our tools into our sensorium. Think of driving a car. All those bodily movements one makes are melded so that we *incorporate* the car. We alter our focus from what feet, legs, hands, arms, and so on are doing, and we attend rather to what our automobiled-body does. Many animals use tools, and some also have abilities to use symbols, but in neither case are the physical or cognitive tools incorporated as in humans. I am reminded of the ideal Zen gardener, whose relationship with the garden is that they are not two and yet not one (see Egan 2000). Our tools are distinct from us yet not distinct—and this is especially true of our cognitive tools.

The most prominent of our cognitive tools is language. We are the ultimate idiots savants of language use. We know from many meditative traditions, particularly (I am reminded by being reminded of the Zen gardener) Buddhist and Zen, how immensely difficult it is to "forget" language, to experience the world freed from the structuring constraints that language lays on our perception. As Chuang Tzu playfully describes the search for human meaning uninfected by words, words, words: "Where can I find a man who has forgotten words so I can have a word with him?" (1996, 140).

My point is that with the accumulation of cognitive tools, such as language, then literacy, then theoretic abstractions, and so on, our ability to learn is enlarged but is also constrained by the tools that are enlarging it, just as the telescope enlarges some particular object by constraining our field of vision. That is, the tools we use, when learning, shape and very largely determine what and how we can learn. So, runs my argument, if you want to understand human learning, you need to understand the cognitive tools that are being deployed in the process. Or, as James Wertsch puts it: "A defining property of higher mental functioning, one which is unique to humans, is the fact that it is mediated by tools and by sign systems such as natural language" (1991, 23).

Let me try an analogy that might underline what I mean. You have to explain how five tons of stones were moved from the mason's yard to the back of a garden. Study of the musculature and skeleton and so on of the human body has exposed fairly precisely what is involved in a person lifting and moving a stone. To try to explain how the five tons of stones got across town in terms of human muscles, bones, joints, sinews, while ignoring the pallet lifter, the truck that drove the stones across the town, the cherry picker that lowered them onto the driveway, and the wheelbarrow that was used to carry them to where they were lifted into place to make a raised garden, would be a bit odd. (The example is currently close to my heart, and closer to my aching knees and back.) It would be even odder if you recognized that the knowledge about muscles, skeletons, and so on could not account for the tonnage moved over the stated distance in the given time and, in response to this recognition, you recommended that more detailed research on muscles, skeleton, and perhaps knees was the way to go in order to solve the problem, still ignoring the truck and other tools. Or, if you want to explain the building of the pyramids in ancient Egypt, you would be unwise to study how their bodies might be able to handle the task while ignoring the uses of hydraulic lifting systems. For Stonehenge, study of the deployment of barges, rollers, and levers might prove more useful than looking for something distinctive about the workers' bodies.

The analogy is supposed to suggest that understanding human learning, especially from the perspective of parents and teachers who want to help children learn, will not likely be much helped by increasingly refined studies of the nature of learning. We would do better to attend to the cognitive tools that students deploy when they learn. In the analogy, the mechanics of the body is equivalent to the nature of learning. We can indeed study how a body lifts and moves stones. Ignoring the truck and wheelbarrow is like ignoring the cognitive shaping that language, literacy, and other symbolic tools give to our learning.

Take language as a major cognitive tool; it in turn breaks down into a set of smaller tools that come along with it. All language users, for example, to take the items Deacon mentioned above, "cannot help but see the world in symbolic categorical terms, dividing it up according to opposed features, and organizing our lives according to themes and narratives." We can see here at least two somewhat distinctive cognitive tools: use of oppositions to gain a conceptual grasp on the world, and use of narrative to shape our experience into emotionally meaningful events. We might go on to explore, for example, how we might represent the world in narrative terms to children for whom this becomes a major tool of learning. It is not a "natural" form of learning; it is a product of deploying an internalized cultural tool that comes along with language. We might make inventories of the cognitive tools we pick up as we grow into particular societies and then consider how these can be used in increasing the effectiveness of children's learning (something I have done in a preliminary way in Egan 1997).

Now obviously our use of these cognitive tools is tied into our "nature." But study of the nature of learning avoids precisely the range of distinctive cultural acquisitions that provides these tools. The tools will differ from culture to culture, whereas researchers who seek to expose the nature of human learning try to exclude those features that seem to be products of cultural conditioning. Researchers have wanted to get "below" these. My point is that there is no there there—or, at least, the accumulation of cultural tools and the profound influence they have on our learning makes it almost impossible, except with pre-language infants, to expose basic principles of natural learning.

The analogy can also take us a little further before breaking down, as analogies are inclined to do. The pallet lifter and the truck and wheelbarrow are all, in one way or another, shaped to respond to the human body. Similarly, underlying the various cognitive tools we deploy there *is* a nature of human learning. When people say, "human beings don't have a nature, we have a culture," they overstate to emphasize a point. The point is that our culture is so powerfully incorporated, and "inmindated," that it is hard to work out just what is our rock-bottom nature or whether our raw nature is accessible under the load of culture. The overstatement is in the suggestion that we don't have a nature. We do, but it becomes harder and harder to determine what it is as we accumulate-inmindate layers of cognitive tools.

We can't avoid having mixed feelings when we discover supporting work that puts more neatly and powerfully what we have been struggling to articulate, especially when it was written three-quarters of a century earlier. The Russian psychologist Lev Vygotsky wrote:

> The inclusion of a tool in the process of behavior (a) introduces several new functions connected with the use of the given tool and with its control; (b) abolishes and makes unnecessary several natural processes, whose work is accomplished by the tool; and (c) alters the course and individual features (the intensity, duration, sequence, etc.) of all the mental processes that enter into the composition of instrumental act, replacing some functions with others (i.e. it re-creates and reorganizes the whole structure of behavior just as a technical tool recreates the whole structure of labor operations). [1981, 139–140]

"Underneath" our culture and our cognitive tools we are, of course, parts of the natural world, but our prodigious cultural development has made it hard for us to understand ourselves in natural terms. The problem in part lies in how cultural tools become cognitive tools for each individual. Vygotsky has been one of the most acute observers of how human beings in their development "internalize" aspects of their cultural and symbolic surroundings. I contend that the cognitive transformations brought on by our internalizing prominent features of our cultural environments offer educators more practical knowledge about learning and cognitive development than the kind of psychology that still dominates educational thinking about these topics.

James Wertsch puts it more comprehensively: "The basic goal of a sociocultural approach to mind is to create an account of human mental processes that recognizes the essential relationship between these processes and their cultural, historical, and institutional settings" (1991, 6). While I have just acknowledged my fault in not having been more alert to Vygotsky, I might similarly acknowledge that Wertsch has already developed the conception of cognitive tools use with great force and clarity (1988, 1991, 1997).

So far I have tried to persuade you that progressivism got two connected things wrong. The first is the belief that in their early play and language acquisition and in picking up "street-smarts" children demonstrate a kind of natural learning that should form a model for how teachers should engage them in learning in school. The second is the belief that the scientific study of the nature of human learning will lead to principles for effective teaching.

The two beliefs are more than casually related, of course. The fact that pretty well everyone concerned with education during the twentieth century believed the second idea is what helped make the first one so persistently persuasive. Even if many teachers still do not make their classroom instruction model the kinds of learning that take place in play and in the child's everyday environment, one doesn't hear their practices defended because they think conforming to "natural" models is a bad idea. Rather, nearly everyone I have had contact with agrees that it would be better to make classroom learning more like "natural" forms but that classroom contexts, curricular demands, and lack of time and energy interfere with that desirable aim.

Well, you might reasonably point out that the first belief has been held only by some of the people some of the time, and anyway, I haven't yet done more than indicate some problems with a doctrinaire adherence to it. In a pragmatic business like teaching, you might further point out, we learn to adapt and adopt practices on the basis of what works rather than on the basis of some theory. You might also reasonably point out that I haven't given you any convincing reason to discard the second belief, especially since it has been accepted by most of the people most of the time. All I've done is offer an analogy about tool use that you might not find altogether convincing as mapping on to our difficulties in understanding human learning.

Also no one is likely going to give up the second belief in favor of a "cognitive tools" approach—especially since the idea may still be entirely vague. What do I mean by cognitive tools? Well, in part I mean what Vygotsky meant, and I have elaborated another part in *The Educated Mind*. Alex Kozulin characterizes them as "those cultural artifacts—signs, symbols, texts, formulae, graphic-symbolic devices—that help individuals master their own 'natural' psychological functions" (1998, 1). I want to show in detail how such large-scale cognitive tools, such as oral language, literacy, and theoretic abstractions, have smaller-scale tools inherent in them, such as—for language—metaphor recognition and formation, story-structure recognition and formation, fantasy, forming binary structures and mediating them, rhyme, rhythm, and meter, and forming mental images from words. Similar sets come along with literacy and with theoretic abstractions. Understanding how these tools shape our learning can give us a better set of principles for improving the effectiveness of students' learning than anything progressivism can provide.

One influence of a focus on such cognitive tools is, to use Kozulin's words: "Rather than a superstructure built on the foundations of psychological functions, educational activity is seen as a process radically changing these very functions" (1998, 16)—a theme Vygotsky elaborated in the 1978 collection *Mind in Society*.

"Tool," of course, is quite an inappropriate term for cognition, but I use it because it has become the conventional one—and because I can't think of a better. Cognitive tools are two sided. They are what we use in thinking, but then we can use them to make further cognitive tools. So Shakespeare, for example, learned a variety of cognitive tools and used them to build a set of sonnets and plays. These creative works in turn can become cognitive tools for others, enlarging and making more abundant the audience's cognitive toolbox and, thereby, their experience of human life. On one side these are cultural tools, and then, once internalized by an individual, they become cognitive tools. Vygotsky has much to say about this process. Perhaps I will add to the rebarbative jargon we are becoming buried under by commonly, in what follows, using the term "cultural-cognitive tools" to capture this ambivalence. James Wertsch refers to "mediated action." He discusses how the "study of mediated action focuses on how humans use 'cultural tools,' or 'mediational means' (terms used interchangeably) when engaging in various forms of action. The cultural tools involved may range from simple mnemonic devices such as marks on a stone to natural language and computers, and the kind of action involved may be socially distributed or carried out by individuals" (1998, 239).

One of Herbert Spencer's influential bequests to modern education, then, has been a sharp, morally tinged distinction between natural and artificial forms of learning and instruction. He inherited the distinction indirectly from Rousseau but shaped it into the form that has remained substantially unchanged since the 1850s. The distinction, and Spencer's representation of the mind as a biological organ—which I'll explore in the next chapter—has encouraged more than a century of research aimed at exposing in detail the nature of human learning and then devising methods of teaching that conform with it. That we still see, early in a new century, the same set of practices that Spencer recommended being promoted as new paradigms and as the implications of the latest research, suggests that something is wrong. What is wrong is the inadequate recognition of how human learning is affected by our cognitive tools.

chapter 3

· ·

DEVELOPMENT,

· ·

PROGRESS, AND THE

· ·

BIOLOGIZED MIND

· ·

That famous autobiographer Jean-Jacques Rousseau wrote that, through the varied scenes of life, a man's interests change such that at "ten his mind was set upon cakes, at twenty it is set upon his mistress; at thirty it will be set upon pleasure; at forty on ambition, at fifty on avarice" (1911, 395). We might consider that this doesn't ideally capture how we would distinguish the main stages of our lives, especially if "we" are women, but it exemplifies a fundamental observation all educators have to make and contend with. Human beings go through a long process of what we now commonly call development; during this process our interests and abilities change in both gross and subtle ways, and there seem to be regularities in the ways people go through the varied scenes of life. The educator's difficult task is to describe these developmental changes, and their regularities and irregularities, and prescribe educational programs that take them into account.

The task is difficult, in part, because prescriptions keep interfering with descriptions. That is, when someone describes "the developmental process," we have to ask how far they are giving us an account of some natural, spontaneous process or how far they are describing a process shaped by our previous educational prescriptions. For example, we routinely prescribe that children should learn to read and write between ages five and seven; if we note regular changes in children's cognitive development a little later, are these changes "natural" or effects of literacy? Is Rousseau's a description of regularities in males' spontaneous development, or is it a description of regularities shaped by the conventions of his time? An interest in mistresses over cakes at twenty might seem a regular and natural product of male puberty, but it is also obviously tied to the social conventions, and exploitations, of the time. Sorting the natural from the cultural shapers of development matters to educators—it has been assumed—because the former is the bedrock on which teaching, curricula, and all the structures of schooling must be built for the institution to succeed. The danger, of course, is that taking descriptions as the basis of our prescriptions can give our supposedly descriptive developmental theories the status of self-fulfilling prophecies.

Educators seem widely to assume that we need to locate that bedrock of development in a spontaneous psychological process, which careful research will be able to expose in increasingly reliable detail. Theories, such as that of Jean Piaget, claim to describe the underlying psychological process of cognitive development whose stages determine what knowledge the developing individual can understand. Educational prescriptions and programs that cohere with such theories are called "developmentally appropriate."

You will be unsurprised by this point that the modern formulation of these ideas finds a prominent source in Herbert Spencer's writings. What Spencer had, that Rousseau lacked, was a theory of evolution that provided a template for thinking about growth and change in a new way. Spencer's ideas about development became central to progressivism and are still very widely believed. These ideas have persisted and play a dominant role in current educational thinking, planning, and practice. Yet they have been wrong from the start and haven't become less wrong for a century and a half of assuming that they're right.

So what is wrong with the considerable industry of research about cognitive development and its educational implications? First, the human mind remains a mysterious country to its possessors. We expand our understanding by using metaphors and analogies. So we ask, "What is the mind like?" The trouble is that the human mind is unlike anything else we know. The first thing that Spencer and modern researchers got wrong was to take too literally the metaphorical answer that the mind is like the body; or, rather, researchers and those who rely on them misjudged the degree of metaphor involved in thinking of the mind in terms derived from thinking about the body.

Spencer wrote, "We must compare mental phenomena with the phenomena most like them. . . . The phenomena which those of Mind resemble in the greatest degree are those of bodily life" (1897, 292–293). As a result of using such an analogy, all kinds of biological notions have been imported into thinking about the mind and its development. The mind became thought about as a kind of organ or organism (Morss 1990). Its "growth" became a focus of effort in education. What, for the mind, is like food for the body? Our metaphor supplies the obvious answer—knowledge! So knowledge is referred to as "food" or "aliments" to mental "growth" by Spencer and Piaget and many others. And, most influentially, the belief took hold that the mind goes through its own spontaneous process of growth, with major changes at specific stages: as the body goes through puberty, so the mind goes through—to use one of Piaget's terms—concrete operations. As a further result, children's thinking is seen as a kind of embryo of adult thinking. The distinctive forms of children's cognition, and especially any superiority in children's cognition, thus tend to become suppressed or ignored or seen only as primitive forms of adult cognition.

Again, the basic idea from which these modern beliefs derive seems to be Aristotle's notion that every living thing has a natural form and that each organism's growth is determined by an innate need to reach the fullest realization of that form. Once the mind is conceived of as a kind of organism, it, too, is thought about in these terms.

A second set of errors that follow from thinking of minds as like bodies concerns the relation such a view sets up between minds and knowledge. Knowledge becomes subservient—an aliment or food —to a supposedly distinct process of mental development. Here's a reason why we might be wary of accepting the knowledge-mind relation set up by seeing knowledge as like food for the mind: "To acquire knowledge is to learn to see, to experience the world in a way otherwise unknown, and thereby come to have a mind in a fuller sense. It is not that the mind is some kind of organ or muscle with its own inbuilt forms of operation, which if somehow developed, naturally lead to different kinds of knowledge. It is not that the mind has predetermined patterns of functioning" (Hirst 1974, 40). From Hirst's viewpoint, the belief that one can locate and describe some underlying process of cognitive development is an illusion. Again, like Gertrude Stein's Oakland, there is no there there. What has been the subject of so much research, Hirst suggests, is simply a byproduct of the kind and amount of knowledge we have learned. If there are regularities to be seen, they are produced by the regularities of our having socialized children and having taught them certain forms of knowledge at regular times.

Hirst's are not the only grounds on which we might worry about modern research on cognitive development. When Jerry Fodor concludes that he is "inclined to doubt that there is such a thing as cognitive development in the sense that developmental cognitive psychologists have in mind" (1985, 35), or when Rom Harré asserts that there "is no internal schedule of [cognitive] maturation that parallels the internally driven schedule of physical development" (Foreword to Morss 1990, xii), we might not be quite so reluctant to consider that the imperial personage of developmental theory is somewhat deficient in the clothing department. A further ground for reaching such a conclusion echoes my argument in the previous chapter: what have commonly been seen as the results of cognitive development might be better seen as the results of people's acquiring and using specific sets of cognitive tools in specific, logically constrained, sequences.

A third set of errors about development derives from Spencer's conception of evolution and how that influenced his, and current, thinking about development. As we saw in Chapter 1, Spencer tied ideas about evolution, development, and progress tightly together. Twentieth-century psychology inherited a conception of development that was complicatedly bound up with a nineteenth-century conception of progress. Modern theories of cognitive development are "hierarchical integrative"—that is, each stage or phase of development contains, elaborates, and builds on the developments of the previous stage or stages. They have the characteristics of progress and consequently do not observe losses that might be entailed in development.

When Chuang Tzu reflected on an aspect of his cognitive development, he wrote that he felt "like a man who, having left home in his youth, has forgotten the way back" (1996, 42). He points to a feature of development that is achingly familiar—one which identifies some loss that comes with the gains. Progressive notions of development ignore its costs. Another aspect of our development that makes us seem like idiots savants is highlighted by such observations as these: "high levels of literacy skills may entail considerable costs, as indeed has been suggested by the literature comparing the cognitive competences of oral cultures with those of literate ones. Oral memory and visual imagery are often listed among the skills that may have been traded off against literacy" (Donald 1993, 746). Later I'll point to a set of further costs involved in our cognitive gains to emphasize how progressivism has confused a crucial feature of our cognitive development. Spencer's nineteenth-century notion of progress has been a worm in the bud of research on cognitive development.

. . . .

SPENCER ON DEVELOPMENT

In 1851, Spencer read a review of W. B. Carpenter's *Principles of Physiology*. In his autobiography half a century later, Spencer describes this review as an "incident of moment" in his intellectual life. The review introduced him to the decades old idea of Karl Ernst von Baer, which we encountered in Chapter 1, that all living organisms develop from a condition of homogeneity to one of increasing heterogeneity. The "incident of moment" was Spencer's recognition that this formula could be applied to the evolution of inorganic no less than to organic material, and to individuals today no less than to species in the past. Indeed, the more he thought about it, the more he concluded that it could be applied to everything! It was Spencer's restrained "Eureka!" He was not the kind of person to run down the street naked, Archimedes-like, shouting his discovery (especially given the English climate), but with proper English reserve he noted that this insight allowed him to link "thoughts that were previously unorganized, or but partially organized" (1881, 337). He had discovered, he thought, a fundamental principle of nature.

By now we are fairly familiar with the steps Spencer took from his general principle to his recommendations for teaching and learning, so I will rehearse them only briefly. Spencer saw in the homogeneous-to-heterogeneous principle a way of organizing his ideas about evolution. Looking back at the emerging fossil record, he saw, from the earliest times, simple-celled creatures, and the gradual increase in complexity over time until, in the present, there were such enormously complex and sophisticated forms of life as, well, Herbert Spencer. With this template of a progressive, unilinear, regular conception of evolution, Spencer found he could successfully apply it also to what he called the "evolution of intelligence" in children. By looking at children's development through his great idea, all the data could be fitted to the general scheme—observations and thoughts that had been previously unorganized or but partially organized suddenly fell into place. From the simplest reflexes of the newborn, he could chart, as with evolution itself, a progressive, unilinear, regular path of increasing complexity to adult rationality.

Spencer's view of development is what today would be called interactionist, but as remains true with most developmental theories today, it is a limited interaction. "Evolution," he wrote, "is commonly conceived to imply in everything an intrinsic tendency to become something higher. This is an erroneous conception of it. In all cases it is determined by the cooperation of inner and outer forces" (Gould 1977, 31). So, too, the child's mind develops in interaction with its environment. This interactionism goes along with the other template Spencer used for thinking about mental development—that of the body's development. The environment provides the required support, stimulation, and food not only for the body but also for the mind. The environment's role in each case is to supply the food that body and mind need to realize their inbuilt goals: adulthood for the body, rationality for the mind.

The educator's task, then, is to recognize that "there is a sequence in which the faculties spontaneously develop, and a certain kind of knowledge which each requires during its development; and that it is for us to ascertain this sequence, and supply this knowledge"

(1928, 52–53). What the good teacher has to do, then, is "to guide the intellect to the appropriate food" (68). The feeding metaphor is extended even to Spencer observing that during early years: "For mental pablum also [the child] is at first dependent on adult aid. . . . Unable to prepare its own food, it is in like manner unable to reduce many kinds of knowledge to a fit form for assimilation" (55). The teacher thus becomes like an environmental aide, or, using Spencer's metaphor, like a domestic servant to the master-program of development inherent in the child's mind.

So, "the mind like the body has a predetermined course of evolution" (1966, 67), and its development involves "slow steps of mental progress that accompany slow steps of bodily progress" (1897, 617). In educating children, we must render "our measures subservient to that spontaneous unfolding which all minds go through in their progress to maturity" (1928, 71). Once we grasp "the leading generalizations of the *science* of mental growth" we can, if we are sensible, devise methods of instruction and curricula that constitute "the chief canons of the *art* of fostering mental growth" (1966, 100).

To get education right, Spencer asserted that we must "consider the course which Psychology dictates" (1928, 65). The primary dictate is that we must "follow the suggestions which the unfolding mind itself gives; facilitating its spontaneous activities, and so aiding the development which Nature is busy with" (65). The belief that psychology would expose nature's plans so that educators could facilitate spontaneous development has been with us for a century and a half now. At the beginning of this tradition of educational inquiry, Spencer announced that such a position supported a number of prominent generalizations—which remain commonly believed today.

Prominent among these generalizations was our old friend homogeneity-to-heterogeneity, mostly referred to in his education writings as "simple to complex." The first generalization or principle we must observe is "the necessary law of progression from the simple to the complex" and that "the progression must be by slow degrees to impressions most nearly allied" (1966, 81, 82). That is, we must begin with what is familiar to the child and then gradually move to slightly less familiar material, expanding the child's understanding by steady degrees. His major generalizations lead to the developmental principle, which we explored in Chapter 2, that we "progress from the simple to the complex, from the indefinite to the definite, from the concrete to the abstract, from the empirical to the rational" (99).

A dilemma for Spencer, and for progressivist educators who have adopted his principles, is the conflict between how easy it ought to be to educate children successfully, given that nature is busy about their proper development all the time, and the conclusion of endless reports and task forces that we aren't doing very well for most children. The common solution offered to this conflict is that natural mental development is not very robust. Although education is properly, in this view, a matter of facilitating a spontaneous process, we have to recognize that the "natural process of mental evolution . . . is not to be disturbed without injury; that we may not force on the unfolding mind our artificial forms; but that psychology, also, discloses to us a law of supply and demand to which, if we would not do harm, we must conform" (Spencer 1966, 46).

. . . .

WHAT IS WRONG?

Three general flaws with progressivist views have created problems in education, and I'll break them down here. Many of the practical uses of progressivist principles considered in the previous chapter might equally well have been put here—concrete to abstract, known to unknown, simple to complex, and so on.

Knowledge as Mental Food

The interactionist view of organisms developing in supportive environments, unfolding and growing according to their inbuilt schedules, makes sense as a characterization of the body's development. Two people may eat quite different foods, but they will usually develop the regular number of arms, legs, toes, and so on; they will not develop to look like the dominant foods in their diet—Mr. Carrot and Ms. Sweet-Corn. It is not clear that our mental development is similarly uninfluenced by the particular knowledge we learn. We don't have to go to the other extreme of seeing the mind as made up *only* of the knowledge it learns, as Paul Hirst recommends we do. That would be to conceive of the mind as a purely epistemological organ. But to see the knowledge we accumulate as supporting psychological development as food supports physical growth seems equally implausible.

When Alfred, Lord Tennyson's Ulysses tells us that among the much that he has seen and known there were those battles "Far on the ringing plains of windy Troy," he adds, "I am a part of all that I have met" ("Ulysses"). We need our developmental theories to account for how the mind's growth incorporates our experience and knowledge not simply as some environment to a more profound and important underlying developmental process, because we recognize that some forms of knowledge and certain experiences shape us or constitute us in important ways. Our experiences are not like foods that are consumed, absorbed, and dissipated in work, waste, and growth; our experiences and knowledge remain as important constituents of our minds. Last night's salmon dinner may have been delicious, but I have not become more salmonlike as a result; my body has absorbed the protein and other nutrients and eliminated what it could not use. But knowledge of those battles on the windy plains of Troy and experience of kayaking among the islands of Masset Inlet are not similarly incidental to the mind's de-

Development, Progress, and the Biologized Mind

velopment. We are a part of all that we have met, and all that we have met remains a part of us.

The metaphor that has given us a biologized view of the mind has also determined how people use the metaphor to think about knowledge. So, while we may conceive of different foods consumed by different people as nevertheless having similar "underlying" nutrients, we may analogously conceive of different knowledge learned by different people as nevertheless having similar "underlying" structures for the mind. Accepting the metaphor that sees the mind as like the body, that is, generates a division of knowledge into two kinds—a surface level at which differences in the range of knowledge individuals hold is evident and an underlying, "structural," level at which common features are to be found. Rousseau did it first, distinguishing between knowledge that is peculiar to each and knowledge that is common to all. Piaget adapted this distinction, calling the superficial knowledge peculiar to each "figurative" and the basic knowledge common to all "operative"—figurative knowledge being the subject of relatively trivial "learning," operative knowledge that of more profound "development."

This is worth laboring over because, although the distinction is built in to psychological research on cognitive development, it rests on nothing more than the metaphoric seeing of the mind as like the body. There is no adequate reason to think that the mind is like the body in these ways; there is no adequate reason to divide knowledge into operative and figurative or common-to-all and unique-to-each; there is no adequate reason to believe that minds go through some predetermined schedule of developmental stages. The main reason that has created this modern view of the mind is an old metaphor.

Now, having said all that, I nevertheless don't want to argue that there is no such thing as mental development or that we can't make useful distinctions among kinds of knowledge. A bit like my view of the "nature of learning" in the previous chapter, there may indeed be an underlying developmental process that determines what and how we can learn about the world. But I am quite sure that recent and current developmental theories are far from describing it adequately; any spontaneous process of cognitive development seems likely to be much less accessible than those based on the kinds of inferences from children's task performance we see currently. If we try to look at the developmental process without the body metaphor shaping our perception, one prominent objection to current theories stands out vividly. Knowledge just doesn't seem to have the same relation with the mind that food has with the body; it constitutes the mind in a way that food doesn't constitute the body. (And this isn't to say that the analogy has no validity, just that it is only an analogy and has commonly been taken as establishing greater similarity between the two processes than is warranted.)

Losses in the Process of Development

The influence of Spencer's general principles has also hidden and falsified those features of children's thinking that are superior to adults'. By seeing the mind as an organ that unfolds progressively, one sees children's intellectual activities *only* in terms of their embryonic relationship to the adult mind. It is a picture of a progressive line, going straight in one direction. So studies of children's abilities to classify objects, for example, themselves classify abilities in terms of the degree to which they approximate the adult ideals of rational, theoretic classification. Nineteenth- and early twentieth-century anthropologists similarly classified people in traditional oral cultures as more or less primitive depending on their use of such intellectual skills as classification according to Western rational norms.

James George Frazer, for example, began his twelve-volume anthropological detective work, *The Golden Bough* (1890–1915), with the image of a priest circling a tree day and night brandishing a flashing sword. "He was a priest and a murderer" (Frazer 1963, 1) because he had earned the priesthood of the goddess Diana's sacred grove at Nemi by killing the previous priest. Any new candidate for the priesthood could gain the office and honor only by killing him. Such was the rule. It was an honor and an office that didn't exactly promote a relaxed lifestyle. Let your guard down or sleep too long at the wrong time, and your successor was on the job. Frazer's desire to uncover an explanation of this curious institution set him on a massive exploration of anthropological lore. And he took a guiding principle of that search directly from Spencer: "In the evolution of thought, as of matter, the simplest is the earliest" (Lévi-Bruhl 1985, 21). Frazer presents the endlessly varied practices he explores as confusions that need careful investigation to sort out and present in rational terms. Thank heavens, he says, for science, after all that "groping around in the dark for countless ages" (1963, 825). The mythologies he had studied so intensively for decades he looked upon "not merely as false but as preposterous and absurd" (vii).

Now I'm not interested either in discounting the values of rationality or in agreeing with Frazer's imperious denigration of mythic thinking, but I am interested in noting, again, how children's thinking still tends to be viewed much as oral cultural thinking used to be seen. Spencer energetically promoted the belief that the "intellectual traits of the uncivilized are traits recurring in the children of the civilized" (1895, 89). Or, as the English leader of the child study movement, James Sully, so confidently put it: "As we all know, the lowest races of mankind stand in close proximity to the animal world. The same is true for infants of the civilized races" (Sully 1895, 395). The American G. Stanley Hall put it more succinctly: "Most savages in most respects are children" (1904, 2:649).

Lucien Lévy-Bruhl, in 1910, was one of the earliest anthropologists to recognize how inadequate it was to classify oral cultural forms of thought as simply "a kind of antecedent stage" (1985, 78) to Western logic. Looking at oral culture in such terms prevented one from seeing what was distinctive and remarkable about the human mind's working in oral traditions. Lévi-Bruhl marveled at the intellectual feats of the people of Australia's outback or northern Brazil. He couldn't begin to compete with their routine powers of memory, for example, "which faithfully reproduces the minutest details of sense-impressions in the correct order of their appearance," and the "wealth of vocabulary and . . . grammatical complexity" of their language use (115).

What I am laboriously trying to point out is that anthropological research exposed early some of the cognitive costs to people in traditional oral cultures of lacking writing and Western rationality. What more slowly has become clear are some of the cognitive costs to people in literate Western cultures of *having* writing and rationality, because of the commitment of intellectual resources they require. "Development," then, is not a matter of inferior versus superior, or simple versus complex in some unilinear hierarchy of intellectual value, as people like Spencer and Frazer assumed; it is rather a matter of trade-offs. I want to show that our individual cognitive development today within Western cultures might be better seen in similar terms—development with trade-offs.

If, instead of seeing children's cognition as simply the embryonic beginning of a process leading to adult rationality, we see it as a result of an evolutionary adaptation to the life tasks that face us at particular times in our development, we might focus better on some of its more distinctive features. Our evolutionary inheritance has ensured for us a commitment of enormous cognitive resources in our early years for orienting ourselves to a complex culturally mediated world. Many cognitive skills that are required for this early orientation reach their peak of energetic activity before age five.

Because most research on children's cognition has presupposed the Spencerian progressive view of development, most attention has been given to identifying the embryonic origins of rational forms of thought and tracing their growth. Relatively little effort has gone toward disclosing those areas of children's cognition that seem superior to adults'. Yet in terms of simple intellectual energy and imaginative productivity, the average five-year-old leaves the average adult limp with exhaustion. When one sees an unsparing (of adult preconceptions) look at modern childhood, such as Cedric Cullingford presents, particularly in his rather disturbing *The Human Experience: The Early Years* (1999), one feels a little shamefaced about one's adult incomprehensions in dealing with children's vivid minds.

One area of children's cognition that seems clearly superior to adults' has been investigated. Metaphor, which "is at the root of the creativity and openness of language" (Winner 1988, 16), seems much more readily generated and recognized by the average five-year-old than by the average adult. Metaphor is important in all flexibility of thinking, not because it is a way of seeing similarities among different things, but because it "creates a similarity [rather] than . . . formulates some similarity antecedently existing" (Black 1962, 83). Metaphor generation seems to go into decline with the onset of schooling and literacy (Winner 1988, 103).

What Ellen Winner describes with regard to metaphor might be extended to imaginative life generally. It is a cliché that young children are vividly imaginative and become more literal and duller during the first few years of schooling. Traditional research on children's imaginative lives is hard to do, but if we had a rich body of such research, it would probably not describe the kind of progressive developmental profiles that Spencer and Piaget have offered us. The profile of the development of imagination in our lives seems quite unlike that ever-rising progress from childhood to adulthood that is represented in hierarchical-integrative, biology-derived developmental theories. Although we lack any precise image of the development of imagination, even the most casual observation of human beings at various ages suggests that it would be absurd to claim that imagination is only embryonically present in young children and becomes increasingly more evident, elaborate, and rich as we age. Give a box to a typical adult and to a typical child and ask them to work out different uses for it; when the adult gives up after a few minutes with six uses, the child is into the fiftieth and just warming up.

If we look at children's imaginative lives, rather than their slowly accumulating logico-mathematical skills, we do not see intellectual activity dominated by the concrete, the simple, the indefinite, the empirical, and so on. We see prodigal metaphoric invention, talking middle-class rabbits, titanic conflicts of good and evil, courage and cowardice, fear and security, and so on.

Of course, we need to be careful not to fall into opposite and sentimental notions of children's "magical" cognition, in reaction against the sort of Spencerian-Piagetian view of children as mental incompetents that has long held sway. And if our process of cognitive development might be better seen as one of constant trade-offs and of losses as well as gains, we need to recognize the great value of what we gain with rationality. The educational value of seeing development afresh in this trade-off sense is that it helps us to recognize what we have all along been sacrificing for our rational gains and perhaps to recognize that we have too often sacrificed more than is necessary or sensible. An alternative metaphor to help us see development in such a trade-off way might be the telescope's ability to enlarge our powers of vision but at the cost always of constraining our field of vision. (In *The Educated Mind,* I show what losses are entailed by each major gain in understanding.)

Incompetent Infants

To pick up a point from the previous chapter: Spencer's conception of development as a unilinear progress from homogeneous to
heterogeneous constructs the newborn as the possessor of some reflexes and senses that are uncoordinated and able to deal only with
the simplest phenomena they respond to. This view of infants as
having virtually no conceptual life—disputed endlessly by parents
whose observations are silent in the research literature—has, during the past quarter century, come tumbling down. Given that we
can't for some reason remember our experience before we become
competent at language, when researching infants' cognition we
have little to go on besides what they can do and what they look at
and how they look at things. They can't do very much, of course,
and, as Mandler puts it, "a good deal of evidence suggests that we
have tended to confuse infants' motor incompetence with conceptual incompetence" (1993, 89). Paying attention to what infants
look at and how they look has yielded evidence of aspects of their
conceptual competence.

The recent revolution in understanding our intellectual beginnings has come about by closely observing what Spencer called the
"vacant stare of the infant" and discovering that it is anything but
vacant. If one bounces a ball, a baby will typically observe it briefly
until distracted by something else. If one rigs up an apparatus that
makes the ball stop in midair or bounce in a manner that doesn't
accord with the laws of motion, the baby will typically stare much
longer at the anomaly. The extended and surprised observation of
the unexpected has helped researchers discover something of what
babies already expect and know.

It had been assumed that babies, from experience and constant
interaction with the environment, gradually come to integrate their
distinct senses of touch, vision, taste, and so on. But if a one-
month-old is habituated to a pacifier with irregular features on the

nipple, is then prevented from seeing it, and next is shown both the irregular pacifier and a smooth one, the baby will stare longer at the irregular one (Meltzoff and Borton 1979). If a three-month-old is shown a rod moving to and fro behind a block of wood, and then the block is removed, the infant will quickly cease to look at the rod moving to and fro by itself. But if the infant is also presented with a rod divided in two with a gap where the block of wood was, the infant will look more intently and longer at the broken rod, indicating that it represents something unexpected (Kellman and Spelke 1983). Related experiments, such as hiding objects behind screens and later retrieving the object from either the screen behind which the infant saw it placed or, by a trick, from behind a different screen, elicit different responses from the infant. More intensive attention is given to the anomaly, suggesting that the infant recognizes it as anomalous. Such cases suggest that, although babies have a lot to learn, they inhabit from the beginning an orderly and stable world and they have precise expectations about how a range of objects should behave.

A baby at four days old already attends to language differently from other sounds. Babies don't gradually learn to distinguish language but recognize from as early as we can discover that language is distinct from all other sounds and is meaningful in a unique way (Mehler et al. 1986). After only a few days' input, babies distinguish their native language from other languages. They recognize faces immediately as sources of special meaning and do not have to learn to distinguish them from some b[l]ooming, buzzing confusion. They differentiate biological from machine motion as early as three months. Our number sense, similarly, does not grow gradually as a result of observing objects; rather, "a predisposition to numerically relevant data is built into the architecture of the human mind" (Mandler and Bauer 1988, 99).

One could go on, and researchers are going on, charting the ways newborn humans come with a brain already organized to make sense of the world. How this complex organ works, how much knowledge it already contains or requires environmental triggers to activate, or how much it is simply a very effective organ for rapidly learning specific knowledge, is still debated. These are issues to be resolved empirically, and they are daily being resolved. What is clear, however, is that Spencer's view of an undifferentiated and intellectually incompetent infant mind is wrong. That wrongness has persisted to the present, built in to developmental theories.

. . . .

INTO THE TWENTIETH CENTURY
WITH JEAN PIAGET

Piaget was by far the most influential theorist dealing with development during the twentieth century, and certainly his influence on developmental aspects of education has dwarfed, and continues to dwarf, everyone else's. Yet his developmental theory embodies most of the wrong ideas we have encountered in Spencer's writings.

Earlier I made much of Spencer's biologizing, and evolutionizing, the mind, claiming that a useful analogy was taken to misleading lengths. There were, of course, many routes by which this idea influenced education during the twentieth century. Lawrence Cremin describes how the "idea of an objective psychological theory firmly rooted in evolutionary biology" (1969, 115–116) was given to John Dewey by William James, and we shall see some of the results of this gift later in this chapter. Piaget, too, echoed Spencer: "The psychological development that starts at birth and terminates in adulthood is comparable to organic growth. . . . Just as the body evolves towards a relatively stable level . . . so mental life can be conceived as evolving toward a final form of equilibrium represented by the adult mind" (1968, 3). (I've never felt "equilibrium" was a particularly apt term for characterizing my adult/addled mind.)

A Brief but Unavoidable Excursus on the Mind

The biologizing of the mind that I have been decrying is precisely, you might reasonably object, one of the conscious triumphs of the modern worldview. It is not some analogy whose limits of usefulness people failed to notice; rather, it was the location of the mind within the biological order that freed us from all that metaphysical and mystical confusion.

Earlier in our cultural history it had been assumed that the mind was a different stuff from the body, and not constrained by the rules of the body. The recognition of the mind as the same stuff as the body was all a part of what people like Frazer celebrated as the triumph of reason and science over uncounted dark millennia of preposterous nonsense. In particular it was a freedom from René Descartes' mind-body dualism and, even more important for education, a freedom from the belief that reliable knowledge could be best achieved by passive contemplation—as exemplified by Descartes sitting in front of his well-stoked fire just working out the truth. In place of this passivity, we have now an understanding that knowledge comes reliably from experiment and so from action on the world. With the biologizing of the mind, human beings could be seen to take our proper place in the natural world—oddly evolved in the brain department but very much a complex biological organism.

My continuing complaint, in response to this, is that the biologizing of the mind has been mistakenly extended and has resulted in diminishing the distinctiveness of the mind's development, seeing it as too much like the body's.

But, you might continue to object, we have good reasons for associating the mind with the brain, and the brain *is* a biological organ that grows and develops as part of the body. So it makes absolute sense to look at the mind as a biological organ subject to analogous developmental processes as the body.

This is all true, but I want still to emphasize that the human mind is indeed odd in the natural world. Among its oddities is that it is has language and deploys cognitive tools in a peculiar way. The hand is not a part of the brain, but is the hand a part of the mind? (When asked, my students all vote yes. I'm not sure why they are all so convinced. When I tell them that their vote has conclusively settled the issue, they do recognize that this isn't how such questions should be decided.) But how about the tools we use? Are the needle and thread or the plane and screwdriver a part of the mind as we work with them? They aren't a part of our brains, but answering whether they become part of our minds is more awkward. Language has enabled us to invent conceptual tools, like the story or the theory, and the narratives and formulas that we elaborate in these forms. Are these parts of our minds? Well, indeed, they seem to become constituents of our minds. So, is mathematics and that Shakespeare sonnet you learned, or ought to have learned, a part of your mind? Yes. A part of your brain? Well—we seem to be turning back on ourselves—given the modern biologized mind, yes. Yet brains are contained within our skulls, whereas minds are oddly composed of things like language that are cultural objects external to our bodies that we come to own or partake in but that we had no part in making and that we share with others.

The difficulty in all this is because the mind "coevolved in close interaction with both brain and culture" (Donald 1993, 737). Using Merlin Donald's terms, the invention of external visuo-symbolic forms "constitutes a hardware change just as real as the biological hardware change" that mediated earlier evolutionary developments of the brain (745). The trick of externalizing aspects of our cognitive functioning—primarily our memory store, but increasingly much else—has transformed "internal" cognitive functions over the past thirty or forty millennia.

Now, our individual internalization of cultural stuff is clearly tied into the ways biological brains develop. The transformations of mental functioning caused over the millennia by our invention and accumulation of cultural stuff is not a biological transformation—culture evolves faster than bodies, as Terrence Deacon has pointed out to interesting effect (1998). Cultural development obviously has to be parasitic on the brain's capacities and must be constrained by how the brain's resources may be exploited and even re-jigged for cultural purposes. But, millennia of accumulated culture later, the transformation of the individual's cognition, as chunks of cultural stuff are learned, is profoundly shaped by the particular cultural stuff itself. Our intellectual evolution, unlike that of other species, has been not in the direction of hardwired modules but rather toward flexibility in the face of change and novel circumstances: "biology has supplied us with the tools to transcend biology" (Skidesky 2000, 27). To use Donald's terms again, if the mind coevolved with both brain and culture, we would be sensible to find a way of thinking and talking about the mind that honors both brain and culture.

I have elsewhere (1997) used terms like "mythic understanding" or "romantic understanding" to capture both sides of the coin of mental development. Such categories acknowledge a biological base of brain development and focus on transformations of cognition brought about by learning cultural stuff. The transformation of individuals' cognition today, after those intellectually energetic millennia, seems to me more clearly seen by exposing the powers that cultural "tools" give to minds than by pursuing an elusive search for some natural psychological reality—to use Piaget's terms— that supposedly undergirds mental development and then drawing inferences to educational practice. We have suffered from tenuous inferences drawn from insecure psychological theories for generations now, without obvious benefit.

Back to the Chase

Piaget became famous because of his surprising explanation of something most people had noticed but had treated as of no particular interest. Countless generations before him had observed that young children commonly held peculiar false beliefs. Piaget's genius was in pointing out that these false beliefs were not things children learn from nature, because the natural world would have instructed them, à la Rousseau, properly. Nor were they things that they had learned from their parents or other adults, who would never have told them, for example, that the number of objects change depending on how you lay them out or that there is more water in a tall, thin vase than in a short, squat one when each actually contained the same amount. Nor were these false beliefs random among children—chaotic froth to be blown away with the rise of reason. Piaget showed that a significant range of beliefs about the natural world, society, dreams, and morality were held in regular ways and changed at regular times through our early lives. His fame became greater as he published increasingly elaborate theories that claimed to explain these beliefs and to describe them as an intelligible part of the process of cognitive development we all pass through on the way to adult rationality. The false beliefs were a key that allowed Piaget to unlock the door to the underlying process of the mind's development. His "genetic epistemology" proposed a new account of the growth of knowledge in humans, replacing Spencer's belief that the environment provided it or others' belief that it must be innate and simply unfold.

Both Spencer's and Piaget's conceptions of development are essentially progressive. Spencer's root metaphor of homogeneous-to-heterogeneous is echoed by Piaget's metaphor of differentiation—"the problem of going from cognitive structures initially undifferentiated . . . to structures both differentiated and coordinated in a coherent way . . . dominates the whole mental development" (1974b, 121). Neither allows for any possibility except a gradually improving mind. This progressive view hides any irregularities, backtracking, or convolutions of our development and cannot accommodate the possibility that young children are intellectually superior to adults in any way. Neither Piaget nor Spencer could make any sense of Charles Baudelaire's famous dictum: "Genius is childhood recaptured." For them, nothing is lost; there are no costs to the mind's development of the rationality they conceive as the fullest realization of the mind's organic growth.

Conceiving mental development as gradual and increasing differentiation, like the body's development from embryo to adult, meant that Piaget also agreed with Spencer's false belief about the condition of the child's mind in early infancy: "At birth, mental life is limited to the exercise of reflex apparatuses" (1963, 9). Piaget claimed that infants between birth and one-and-a-half to two years are involved with perceptual and motor functioning that lacks a representational or conceptual dimension. Recent research on infants' cognition has undermined this part of the Piagetian theoretical edifice. As Mandler rather conservatively puts it, "the theory of an exclusively sensorimotor stage of development . . . is in need of considerable revision" (1993, 89). (I don't want to engage here in an extended critique of Piaget's work—been there, done that, Egan 1983—especially since everyone now seems to be putting the boot in; one of the more devastating and detailed critiques, though, remains Susan Sugarman's, 1987. I want to show just a few of the many cases in which Piaget shared Spencer's false beliefs about cognitive development that are important for education.)

As with Spencer, but more mutedly, Piaget sees a genetic recapitulationary component determining development, and he frequently draws comparisons between children's "spontaneous" theories about, say, the physical world and those of ancient peoples or oral cultures. In his attempts to study "genetic epistemology"—the formation and meaning of knowledge—he felt that "the most fruitful, most obvious field of study would be reconstituting human history—the history of human thinking in prehistoric man" (1971, 13). This source of information isn't available, but that is no problem because "there are children all around us" (13).

Piaget's progress-dominated theory also leads him to support those familiar Spencerian principles about moving from the simple to the complex, the concrete to the abstract, the empirical to the rational, and so on. What Piaget tried to do that Spencer didn't was chart out the gradual growth step by step from the infant's undifferentiated mind to richly differentiated adult rationality. He tried to sketch detailed answers to such questions as "What conceptions of the world does the child naturally form at the different stages of development?" (1967, 61), thereby exposing "the natural psychological reality in terms of which we must understand the development of knowledge" (1964, 9). Unsurprisingly, given their fundamental theoretical agreements, the educational principles derived from Piaget's work are pretty much the same as those proposed by Spencer, the main difference being in the details of the stages Piaget worked out.

Mental development proceeds, according to Spencer and Piaget, by the mind's interactions with the environment, in which the environment provides aliments to the mind. Like food for the body, the aliments do not shape the mind; they can facilitate or hinder its development depending on their appropriateness at particular stages. So teachers can be effective, they both claimed, only if they understand the nature of the developmental process and recognize that their teaching must be "subordinated to spontaneous and psychological development" (Piaget 1970, 716). Both saw the common failures to achieve satisfactory adult rationality as due to the incompetence of teachers and educational institutions. Failures to learn and "develop" are too common, but, Piaget echoes Spencer, "it is not the child that should be blamed . . . but the school, unaware as it is of the use it could make of the child's spontaneous development, which it should reinforce by adequate methods instead of inhibiting as it often does" (Piaget 1961, 11).

This conclusion is justified because they both believed that we have two kinds of learning—one that leads to important developmental changes and the other that is relatively trivial and leads to no significant mental development; one is common to all, the other is particular to each, as their predecessor Rousseau put it. Piaget shows little interest in individual children; as Susan Sugarman has noted, his interest is in "the epistemic subject or cognitive core that is common to all subjects at the same level" (1987, 57). The more profound, common, developmental learning is something that children construct for themselves; it is not subject to instruction. Spencer claimed that, consequently, we should recognize all important education as "self-education," and this profound learning is what "every boy gathers for himself' (1966a, 76). Piaget similarly claimed that the most basic learning is made up of "what the child learns by himself, what none can teach him and what he must discover alone" (1973, 2).

I could go on, for pages and pages, charting similarities—but I hear you cry for mercy and, feeling merciful, will just note that these similarities might be less surprising if we recall the descent with modifications that occurred when Spencer's ideas evolved through the American James Mark Baldwin, who worked in Paris with the French psychologist Pierre Janet, who in turn profoundly influenced the young Jean Piaget. Not, obviously, a unilinear progress, but suggestive of living connections.

Susan Sugarman's observation remains substantially true: "De-

spite appearances to the contrary, Piaget's ideas and overall approach continue to dominate much of developmental psychology"
(1987, 241). Development is still conceived as a largely unlinear
process of increasing differentiation that recognizes no losses attached to cognitive gains; the natural, spontaneous foundation of
psychological development is still assumed to be relatively easily lo-
cated via children's performances on tasks or their verbal responses
to researchers' questions in which "cultural factors" can be "controlled"; the mind is still conceived on the model of other biological
organs with a genetically determined program of growth that we
can isolate and describe. I think that all these basic beliefs of developmental psychology are false.

But whatever may be the case in psychology, Piaget's ideas and
overall approach absolutely dominate in education. Even as Piaget's
name is less evident in curriculum documents justifying inclusion
of particular topics or instructional methods, the influence of his
theory has become unquestioned (Roldão 1992). "Development" in
education is discussed and taught, in my experience and informal
surveys, almost exclusively in Piagetian terms. His progressive stage
model— despite recent research and theoretical attacks— is taught
to students as simply how things are; they have to recognize these
stages of development and their characteristics so that they can
facilitate students' cognitive development. Before school boards
across North America, and in courtrooms in our litigious times, arguments are made for including or excluding topics from the curriculum on the grounds that they are or are not "developmentally
appropriate"; the criterion of appropriateness is invariably Piaget's
model.

In one case, a school board banned books that described same-
sex couples. Some teachers challenged the ban, and a court case en-
sued. The central battle was not, ostensibly, about the "lifestyle"
issues but was focused on the claim that the materials were not "de-

velopmentally appropriate." This claim was supported by a number of psychologists, who cited Piaget's theory as establishing this "fact."

Time to recognize that the emperor is sartorially a tad deficient, we might conclude. But it isn't that easy. The difficulty I find in suggesting problems with Piaget's theory, even though inadequacies might be conceded in point after point, is that it has become the lens that most people in education see children's development through. It is what most educators think about development *with*, and consequently they find it very hard to think *about* its adequacy. Even though theoreticians might represent the theory as a slightly bizarre and baroque edifice constructed on flimsy foundations and researchers are kicking away those foundations, the theory has become like a presupposition, or, as Beatrice Webb tried to reassure Spencer in his final illness, the ideas have "become part of our mental atmosphere" in education.

In general, as I've argued elsewhere (1983), Piaget's theory has been used in education largely as a theory about what children cannot do: "Generations of schoolchildren, deprived of challenging tasks because Piaget said they were incapable of them, bear the evidence of his impact" (Fernández-Armesto 1997, 18). This, of course, reflects Piaget's low opinion of children's intelligence—an opinion he shared with Spencer.

But a part of his appeal to educators, it is easy to underestimate because it may seem silly, is that the details of Piaget's theory look like knowledge. In a field that is rather short on knowledge, here was a theory with a technical language and neat stages that could be taught to students, and students could be tested and graded on how well they had learned it. Another reason for the persistence of Piaget's influence, which may also be underestimated because it is a bit silly, is that he wrote so much and in such a peculiar style that whenever critics suggested errors, they would be told that they had misunderstood Piaget and that, anyway, he had elsewhere made a counterpoint. A rather brusquer, and perhaps excessively unkind, way of explaining the lack of impact of criticism of the theory is: "He published so much, written at such daunting length, in such difficult language and such a tiresome style, that few rivals could read or understand it all. Gradually, many of his observations have been shown to be mistaken, many of his inferences false and most of his influence baneful" (Fernández-Armesto 1997, 18).

. . . .

SPENCER'S, DEWEY'S, AND PIAGET'S DEVELOPMENTAL IDEAS IN PRACTICE TODAY

We needn't inquire very earnestly to see practices in schools today that are direct implementations of Spencer's and Piaget's ideas about development. Again, I don't mean that Spencer or Piaget is the unique and only source of those ideas but that wrong ideas we have seen clearly argued for in their writings are found ubiquitously in our schools today. Given the influence Piaget has had promoting closely similar ideas to Spencer's—though greatly elaborated and jargonized—we can find all kinds of practices justified as "developmentally appropriate" that are based on the flawed foundations I have been poking at here. Let me, instead of shooting those fish in a barrel, show a connection between Spencer's "incident of moment" reading that review of Carpenter's *Principles of Physiology,* with its erroneous eureka, and the currently dominant form of the social studies curriculum. I think this is especially worth looking at because challenges to traditional social studies by those who wish to reintroduce history in the early grades have been countered, in academic journals and in court cases, with the claim that history is "developmentally inappropriate" in the early years and that social studies is ideally developmentally appropriate.

We have seen one major foundation for this curriculum topic in Spencer's developmental beliefs about children's manner of gradually building knowledge from what is most familiar to material that is less familiar.

The principle had two distinct resonances for Spencer and for those who formed the social studies curriculum. First, the knowledge with which young children arrive at school is assumed to be that efficient, reliable, "natural" learning we want to see replicated in schools, and second, the content of that knowledge is the simple, concrete, and empirical material gained from fundamentally meaningful interactions with the child's local environment.

The educational reformers of the late nineteenth and early twentieth centuries encouraged teachers to rethink their ways of presenting new material to students in accordance with this principle — so elementary mathematics would begin from the experience children will have had with fruit or marbles, and language studies will begin with the forms of expression with which children would already be familiar, rather than with abstract grammar. But those subjects were still not fully articulated with the meaningful daily interactions of children in their local environments. What was proposed was a new, central curriculum area — the social studies — which would begin with the material of children's everyday experience, with themselves and their families, their neighborhoods and communities, and gradually expand learning from this meaningful core of students' experience to less familiar knowledge, until, in the end, the whole universe of knowledge could be understood as an expansion from what was most vivid and meaningful to the child. Social studies was designed to tie all the knowledge being learned in other curriculum areas to the child's experience.

So we must start with what is most profoundly known by the student, and build new knowledge on that basis. In North America, Spencer's ideas are best known through John Dewey's formulations of them, and I shall briefly sketch Dewey's echoes of Spencer's mistaken ideas that have supported the social studies.

Let us begin with the fundamental similarities William James noted: "Like Spencer's philosophy, Dewey's is an evolutionism. . . . Like Spencer, again, Dewey makes biology and psychology continuous. 'Life,' or 'experience,' is the fundamental conception" (James 1988, 1136–1137). So it "is a cardinal precept of the newer school of education that the beginning of instruction shall be made with the experiences learners already have" (Dewey 1963, 74), and it is "essential that the new objects and events be related intellectually to those earlier experiences, and this means that there be some advance made in conscious articulation of facts and ideas" (75).

Spencer's insistence that one begins with the empirical is echoed in Dewey's claim: "What is here insisted upon is the necessity of an empirical situation as the initiating phase of thought" (1966, 153); consequently the "true starting point of history is always some present situation with its problems," and "local or home geography is the natural starting point" (214, 212).

They also share a belief that young children can deal only with simple, practical, local, and what Piaget called sensori-motor knowledge: "The knowledge which comes first to persons, and that remains most deeply ingrained, is knowledge of *how to do*; how to walk, talk, read, write, skate, ride a bicycle, and so on indefinitely" (Dewey 1966, 184). This conclusion of the principle seems so patently false that it is bewildering to see it constantly repeated— four-legged flies again. Before, and after, we can walk or skate, we know love and hate, power and powerlessness, the rhythms of expectation and satisfaction of hope and disappointment. The knowledge that comes first and remains most deeply ingrained is not knowledge of "how to do." The knowledge that comes first and remains most deeply ingrained is the fundamental categories upon which we learn to make sense of the world. If our concern is education, the focus on "how to do" is a poor foundation for a process that concerns the development of conscious understanding.

We find Spencer's, and Rousseau's and Piaget's, distinct kinds of learning echoed in Dewey's binary opposition between that which is spontaneous and occurs from interactions with the everyday environment, which "is natural and important," and that artificial instruction that goes on in schools, which "easily becomes remote and dead" (1966, 6, 8). Yes, of course, we can all recognize the difference between learning something profoundly important in our everyday environment and the drone of a dull pedagogy. We can also recognize the difference between a dreary day in our too-familiar local environment and a teacher who opens our eyes to exciting new worlds simply by talking. The point is that the dogmatic way of making this distinction by Spencer and Co. was the product of a cosmology and theories that are false. We do not have to make *this* the decisive way of distinguishing kinds of learning. Indeed, if we want to be sensible, we have to *not* make this the decisive way of distinguishing kinds of learning.

Dewey and Spencer, with their evolutionary conceptions of mental development, have to begin with the simple, the concrete, and the empirical. And they have to work by gradual degrees following a "progressive order, using the factors first acquired as a means of gaining insight into what is more complicated" (Dewey 1966, 20). "Recognition of the natural course of development" (114) is, of course, crucial, and its beginnings are in action, in "learning by doing," and so the young child is conceived to be pretty mindless. These principles have given us the elementary schools we have, in which children are commonly sentimentalized but basically treated as though they can't really think; they can only *do*—so we have all those "hands-on" activities while their huge intellectual energy is hardly engaged with anything significant in the wider cultural world.

The process that Spencer and Piaget characterize as moving from the empirical or sensori-motor to adult rationality, Dewey breaks into three stages. First children learn the "power to do"; second, "this material gradually is surcharged and deepened through communicated knowledge and information"; and, last, "it is enlarged and worked over into rationally or logically organized material" (1966, 184).

So, deploying this set of ideas we get the elementary social studies curriculum that has been largely unchanged since the early decades of the twentieth century: In kindergarten the child begins with herself or himself— (When did you get to know yourself? "At the end of all our exploring," as T. S. Eliot put it) — then they look at families, then neighborhoods, larger communities, interactions among communities, and, so on, expanding gradually outward by steps of "material nearly allied." Why, you might wonder, does this expansive line of associations seem to have a quirky intrusion at about grade four, when children typically study "Indians" or an aboriginal culture in social studies? In Dewey's terms:

> Recourse to the primitive may furnish the fundamental elements of the present situation in immensely simplified form. It is like unraveling a cloth so complex and close to the eyes that its scheme cannot be seen, until the larger courser features of the pattern appear . . . and by seeing how these were solved in the earlier day of the human race, form some conception of the long road which has had to be traveled, and of the successive inventions by which the race has been brought forward in culture. [1966, 215]

Most educators in North America and Australia still seem to believe in the efficacy of the elementary social studies curriculum, as a result of their belief in the ideas on which it is founded. It is, after all, the curriculum that most directly embodies the most basic principles that Spencer, and Dewey, enunciated. What should we expect from a curriculum area designed to conform most precisely with how children's minds develop? There seem to be no grounds for believing that things have changed since Ralph Tyler's 1965 judgment that the social studies are the least effective educationally of any of the basic areas taught in the American public schools. The kinds of tests of students' knowledge of the subject matter of social studies on which that judgment was based continue to show the same discouraging results. Social studies also continues in survey after survey to rank as least popular with students. How can the subject that most directly embodies Spencer's and Dewey's principles be such a mess in practice? Easy—the principles are wrong.

A while ago I mentioned to a colleague whose area of interest is education in the arts that I was trying to get some handle on "development." He said that the subject also interested him and that he had recently read a number of books on moral development, including Piaget's and Lawrence Kohlberg's work. But, he said, they hadn't helped explain the phenomenon that had got him wondering about the subject. "When I teach pottery-making, the five-year-olds work enthusiastically, and give me their work when they finish. With the fifteen-year-olds, I have to do all the work and then they steal it." And Chuang Tzu's observation about how we increasingly "forget the way home" as we grow older isn't enlightened by focusing on the components of "formal operations." Rousseau's stages from cakes at ten to avarice at fifty is more dyspeptically reflected in Kazuko Okakura's "developmental theory": "Man at 10 is an animal; at 20 a lunatic; at 30 a failure; at 40 a fraud; at 50 a criminal" (1989, 117)—well, it works for me.

Of course, these impressionistic reflections have no impact on a self-consciously scientific psychology's theories of development. We moved away from these kinds of observations in the direction of rigorous inquiries when we recognized the mind as like the body. By building in the nineteenth century, and elaborating through the twentieth, a biologized psychology, researchers escaped from the excesses of Cartesian dualism and brought a new methodological rigor to the study of the mind. It managed this, unfortunately— and the point of the previous paragraph's whimsies—by displacing from its subject matter much of what we most want to know about our odd minds. Much of what is most distinctively human in learning and development has been suppressed by the search for the biologized nature of the mind. That search has avoided the cultural stuff that seems to constitute the mind and is not particularly amenable to study by research methods devised to deal with the natural world. We seem to have been saved from the errors of Cartesian dualism at the cost of inadequately recognizing that mind-stuff does have features that are somewhat distinct from body-stuff; that in some degree, the mind is not an Aristotelian organism naturally reaching some maturity inherent in its nature. The dominant position that psychology has held in educational thinking consequently seems to me to have been, and continues to be, a bit of a disaster.

If, instead, we take a "cognitive tools" approach to development, we cease to look for some underlying spontaneous process within physical and cultural environments whose role it is to support some unfolding ontogenesis. Rather, we will see development in the micro scale as "it reveals itself in the restructuring of the child's thinking and behavior under the influence of a new psychological tool"; in the macro scale, development "manifests itself as the life-long process of the formation of a system of psychological functions corresponding to the entire system of symbolic means available in a given culture" (Kozulin 1998, 16). From a Vygotskian perspective, our intellectual abilities are not "natural" but are socio-cultural constructs. They are not forms of intellectual life that we are programmed in some sense to bring to realization; there is no naturally preferred form of human intellectual maturity. We are not designed, for example, to move in the direction of "formal operations" or abstract thinking or whatever. These forms of intellectual life are products of our learning, "inmindating," particular cultural tools invented in our cultural history.

chapter 4

· ·

THE USEFUL

· ·

CURRICULUM

· ·

The tough voices that command attention when educational policy is debated discuss education in terms of economic competitiveness, of endangered citizenship, of the social problems of inner cities, of gun-lack-of-control and reproductive-lack-of-control, of preparation for a digital age, of national cohesion and identity, and so on. The curriculum is represented as an agent of the economy, of civic virtue, of political responsibility, of technological progress, and of much else. That these seem obvious and sensible ways to think about education is an index of the triumph of another set of ideas that Herbert Spencer, among others, promoted.

The process of setting up the new schools for all children in democratic states focused attention on what those children should be taught. The old "ornamental" curriculum, based on classical languages, literature, and history, supposedly designed to enable aristocrats to use their leisure enjoyably, came in for much derision. Spencer broached the topic early and compellingly, and provided his own less than compelling answer in his essay "What Knowledge Is of Most Worth?" (1859).

With his usual brio, Spencer argued that we must sweep away the dominant curriculum: "Men dress their children's minds as they do their bodies, in the prevailing fashion" (1928, 2). Instead of following fashions, we need to begin by considering what is most important in life and prepare children for that. What is most important? Well, he ranked in order: self-preservation, securing the necessaries of life, bringing up children well, producing good citizens, and, last, "those miscellaneous activities which fill up the leisure part of life, devoted to the gratification of the tastes and feelings" (7). (You can still feel his distaste for these last frivolities.) And what knowledge will best support these aims for education? The new scientific knowledge relevant to each, replied Spencer.

Though Spencer meant "science" in the widest sense, most of his followers found his answer too narrow. If his answer was not widely accepted, his question was almost universally agreed to be timely and the right one for designers of a new and modern curriculum for a democratic era. Theorists also accepted that his way of going about answering the question was right—that is, that the ultimate criterion for selecting content for the curriculum must be its utility in the projected life of the student.

Spencer's was obviously not the first or only voice demanding that the curriculum should consist of what would prove most useful to students and society. This was, after all, the first great educational idea, shaped in oral cultures long before. John Locke gave it a more modern, sensible, and bourgeois shape. Reflecting on the best curriculum for the boy whose father he was advising, Locke noted that "since it cannot be hoped he should have the time and strength to learn all things, most pains should be taken about that which is most necessary, and that principally looked after which will be of most frequent use to him in the world" (1964, 47). What Spencer added to this was a claim on the authority of science and modern efficiency in determining precisely what children would need. And he wrote during the heyday of Utilitarianism.

So the prevailing curriculum based on Greek, Latin, and history was to be swept away. This took some time, but it has pretty well gone. In general, Spencer despised the classical bent of the education that had shaped most of his middle-class contemporaries. This education provided a mass of irrelevant knowledge: "So terribly in our education does the ornamental over-ride the useful" (1928, 14). Advocates of future utility as a determining criterion for the curriculum became increasingly influential in the twentieth century. So social studies generally replaced traditional history, classical learning of any kind largely disappeared in favor of more utilitarian studies, the arts in general gave ground to practical preparations for everyday life, literature received less time than functional literacy activities, science and technology studies became a staple of the curriculum, and so on.

Whether we applaud or bewail or have mixed feelings about these changes, it is useful to pause and place them in a wider context that might help us see them more clearly. For the nineteenth- and early-twentieth-century arguments are new forms of those Plato had with the teachers of rhetoric when he introduced his new idea of education. The rhetoricians of the fifth and fourth centuries B.C. had devised a curriculum that included whatever was considered most useful in preparing the young for their future life in society. Spencer continued the tradition of Isocrates, the rhetorician who is the implicit target of Plato's *Republic*. Spencer's scientific and utilitarian curriculum was the new form of rhetoric in its ancient quarrel with philosophy. What we see in the triumph of Spencer's ideas in the state schools of the twentieth century is the significant eclipse of Plato's idea. The new form of rhetoric, the utilitarian curriculum, appealed to politicians and the administrators of the great institutions of modern states because it made the schools very largely into agencies of socialization.

It seemed obvious to Spencer that everyone would agree on the most important features of our existence. At the level of stratospheric generalities it was easy to get consensus that self-preservation, producing good citizens, and so on, were desirable aims. That these, as criteria, could be adapted so readily to devising new American curricula that supported social ideals he despised indicates how such generalities are at the mercy of extremely varied interpretations.

And what have we sacrificed for the useful curriculum? The traditionalist response is that we have lost any sense of an "education whose definition and justification are based on the significance of knowledge itself, and not on the predilections of pupils, the demands of society, or the whims of politicians" (Hirst 1974, 32).

I read the other day about the poet Joseph Brodsky teaching a class at a leading American college and coming to a reference to Ovid. He asked who was familiar with the reference. No one. A suspicion sneaked up on him: Who had heard of Ovid? No one. (A town in upstate New York, isn't it?) He stood stunned, looking at this group of highly intelligent young people, and could say only, "You've been cheated." Cheated out of an education by those who accepted Spencer's criteria—so goes the traditionalist response. But there is *something* in that response, and modern progressivists like Howard Gardner, say, try to show how progressivist ideals and a substantial education in traditional disciplines *can* go hand in hand (such as Gardner 1999). The problem has been, however, that the utilitarian criteria ensure that consumer education, "critical thinking," "problem solving," parenting skills, and "skills" in general (Barrow 1990) will always trump a disinterested pursuit of "irrelevant" knowledge.

Rejecting Spencer's criterion of usefulness does not mean that we have to embrace uselessness. One of Lenin's good lines, when freedom was promoted as an unquestioned good, was to ask, "Freedom for whom to do what?" When people promote usefulness as a guide for our curricula, we might ask, "Useful for whom to do what?" Some of the answers we would be compelled to give for the useful modern curriculum don't bear comfortable reflection. Corporate groups who agitate for an increase in schools' efficiency, for example, may work on behalf of utility all right, but it is a utility that is often not very useful for the development of students' minds, except in a narrow sense. And the eagerness of computer companies to persuade educators that every child needs to be hooked up to the Internet promotes a kind of activity that may be of only marginal educational value, displacing activities of much greater worth.

Below, I lay out those ideas of Spencer's that have been influential in shaping the modern curriculum—recognizing that Spencer was often not their originator or sole advocate or sometimes not even their most effective advocate. Then I'll show what is wrong with these ideas, tracing influential expressions of those ideas through the twentieth century.

. . . .

SPENCER'S CURRICULUM

On 3 October 1892, Laurence Housman attended his brother's inaugural lecture as professor of Latin at University College, London. Many years later Laurence wrote a brief biography of the professor and, more famously, the poet, A. E. Housman, and described a memorable feature of that first lecture: "I then had the amusement of hearing the shocked 'Tut-tuts' with which some of the students greeted his slighting reference to the utilitarian view of education taken by Mr. Herbert Spencer, who was more highly thought of in those days than he is now, but who had always been A.E.H.'s particular *bête noire.* One of his College friends told me that when at Oxford he was already casting scorn on Spencer's claim to be regarded either as a philosopher or a thinker deserving of respect" (Housman 1969, 64). (A. E. Housman's scorn was of heroic proportions, as revealed by his many hilarious and contemptuously dismissive footnotes and his crushing comments on those unfortunate enough to attract his critical attention: one writer's "self love is a great passion squandered on an unworthy object"; Jowett's translation of Plato "the best translation of a Greek philosopher which has ever been executed by a person who understood neither philosophy nor Greek"; and "the faintest of all human passions is the love of truth"; for these and others, see Page 1983, 143–161.)

In this lecture Housman criticized not only Spencer's arguments that we should make our curriculum one of scientific knowledge because it was the most useful area of study but also Matthew Arnold's arguments that the study of humane letters should constitute our curriculum because the culture represented in them would transform our inner nature. Housman conceded that there are more important and certainly more pleasurable things in life than acquiring knowledge, but knowledge provides, he asserted, "the least perishable of pleasures; the least subject to external things, and the play of change, and the wear of time" (Page 1983, 69).

Well, the point of mentioning Housman's inaugural lecture is to recognize the high regard in which Spencer's views were still held around the turn of the twentieth century—those "shocked 'Tut-tuts'" —and the hostility to them by those who rejected Spencer's utilitarian conception of education. We might expect professors of Latin to be hostile to Spencer. An implication of Spencer's writings was that the classics should disappear from the experience of middle-class students and should have no role for the increasing numbers of children from the lower classes who were filling the expanding state schools. The successful realization of Spencer's principles meant that education in the new century could be thought of as needing the classics not at all. Today, of course, the educational establishment—almost entirely without any knowledge of what once was the backbone or staple of education and almost invariably ignorant of classical languages—takes it for granted

that the classics should be treated as an occasional and exotic op-
tion for only a few students. The common view of educationalists
today is that this shift away from the classics marks a triumph of
common sense, a democratization of education, and a recognition
that schooling is properly both a preparation for the everyday life
all classes of students will lead in adulthood and an expansion
of their experience in the present. The less common view, held often by those with a classical education, such as Housman or, say,
Michael Oakeshott, is that this shift has caused an educational
catastrophe by cutting off modern generations from the great conversation of the Western tradition. The product of this move, they
believe, is the condition of modern schooling in which few become
educated and many become socialized—the "You've been cheated!"
response.

Spencer's ideas about the curriculum are not, of course, distinct
from his ideas about learning and development, so we have already
encountered many of the main principles that would shape his curriculum, and the rest may be stated quite briefly. His primary principle is that the content of the curriculum should serve the main
purposes of life. Education, after all, is about how best to live—a
topic on which general agreement has not been conspicuous. But
the best guide and help we can find, in Spencer's view, is science.
This principle, and Spencer's interpretation of it, leads him to such
arguments as: because "the biographies of monarchs . . . throw
scarcely any light upon the science of society" (1928, 26), children's
study of society should focus on what has been exposed by the new
sciences of descriptive or comparative sociology, in a form suitable
to their age. So he argued, as we saw in the previous chapter, for
something like what became social studies. On the same principle
of utility, he argued for the displacement of ancient languages in favor of modern languages, and for the modern languages to be
learned by the same methods a child uses in learning a native lan-

guage. What we now call "immersion" methods were to displace the grammar-based method.

He was an energetic advocate of science in the curriculum, joined by Thomas Huxley in Britain and Charles Eliot in the United States, and the currently common belief that science ought to have a significant place in every student's education is a mark of their success. Spencer also argued for an increase in mathematics, focused on what students would need in their everyday lives.

We have already seen something of the influence of his evolutionary ideas. With regard to the curriculum, the claim that children must begin with local, concrete experience and the simplest elements of each subject means that they will begin each topic in a way that is "purely experimental" (1928, 62). So the curriculum of the early years will be largely one of "sensible experience" (3) and devoid of academic content, of abstraction, of complexity, and of rational activity. It will move toward these in each subject. So we will have no grammar or other abstract subjects in the early years of students' education.

Spencer was mainly concerned to establish overall principles and did not specify their curricular implications in detail, giving only occasional examples. But one can fairly easily work out a Spencerian curriculum. He does also give us an additional principle that is a tad discordant with a number of his specific suggestions, however. He points out that if one is adequately attentive to children's nature and the food their growing minds require, we shouldn't need to "trouble ourselves about any *curriculum* at all" (1966, 67). (This idea was picked up energetically by certain radical voices of the 1960s such as Neil Postman and Charles Weingartner, as I'll discuss later.) In Spencer's view, the educator's task is to aid "self-evolution" (85), and we can easily improvise a curriculum if we remain sensitive to the nature of the child and his or her needs.

The other main principle Spencer drew on to guide the construction of the curriculum was recapitulation. A defining feature of Spencer's curriculum is that it carries "each child's mind through a process like that which the mind of humanity at large has gone through" (1928, 51). So we need only look to the history of how our knowledge grew gradually from primitive beginnings to the present and design our curriculum accordingly. So we should look at how the various sciences began in the unfocused perceptions and earliest experiments of "savages" and follow their gradual systematization to modern times—and an ideally rational curriculum for producing ideally rational people will result. Recapitulation, as a determining principle for the curriculum, has fared least well of all Spencer's educational ideas.

Among his developmental ideas, one has had considerable impact. His hostility to "the forcing-system" and to "precocity" was due to his belief that "formal instruction, far too soon commenced, is carried on with but little reference to the laws of mental development" (1966, 30). His curriculum would be cautious of introducing knowledge for which the child is not ready. This principle is potentially, and has been in practice, a recipe for making the early years of schooling intellectually barren. It was prominent among John Dewey's concerns, as we shall see, and was given a further patina of science by Jean Piaget.

Schemes for the curriculum are commonly a covert form of autobiographical writing. Those eager to propose curricula tend to recommend practices that will shape children to become like themselves—without the defects they might be ready to acknowledge. (This doesn't apply to me, of course.) Spencer is an embarrassingly obvious example of this tendency. His own peculiar education by his father and uncle focused almost exclusively on making him a scientist. He learned little history, had scant acquaintance with modern or classical literature or with the arts, never studied Latin or Greek or grammar, and unsurprisingly, he recommends a similar curriculum for everyone else to replicate his particular form of human perfection.

He was unsympathetic to styles of life unlike his own. It wasn't just savages and peasants he held in contempt, along with so many of his middle-class contemporaries, but he included in his dismissive sweep the rural worker whose idea of pleasure was "sitting in a tea-garden smoking pipes and drinking porter" (1904, 2:87). The squire comes in for contempt, too, because he typically thinks of woods as a place to shoot in, considers all uncultivated plants weeds, and classifies animals as game, vermin, or stock. To Spencer, of course, woods are places to observe and classify species of plant, animal, and insect according to scientific principles—not places for either shooting or idle loitering.

Regretting the frivolity and time-wasting of so many of his contemporaries, Spencer declared that he didn't have time for literature: "Novels were temptations to be resisted; for I dare not expend on them the needful amount of reading power" (1904, 2:263). One may see his particular philistinism most clearly in his comments on art. His theory of progress led him to the conclusion that intellectual evolution must lead to increasingly precise representation in art (1888, 535). So he considered Raphael, Michelangelo, and other Old Masters vastly inferior to his contemporaries' sentimental and semiphotographic pictures in all their admirable natural science accuracy. The Old Masters expressed what to a modern sensibility like Spencer's could be seen only as "crude ideas and sentiments and undisciplined perceptions" (1904, 2:219). Well, one doesn't want to make too much of tastes in art, but it might give us pause to consider that this very oddly educated person, with his eccentric ideas and ignorance of vast areas of human experience, articulated a set of principles for the design of curricula that have considerably influenced modern schooling.

But in conclusion, we should note that Spencer's conception of utility was rather different from that of people who saw the new schools as simply training institutes "for the business of life" (1966, 87). He was harshly critical of such a crude notion of what was useful; if we accept such a view "then indeed it is needless to learn anything that does not directly help to replenish the till and fill the larder" (87). We have higher faculties, he assures us, than the acquisitive and the sensual, and children taken out-of-doors and instructed rationally about nature will spontaneously move toward "those great generalizations of science by which actions may be rightly judged" (88).

. . . .

WHAT IS WRONG WITH SPENCER'S CURRICULUM?

In what follows, I focus on errors that persist today, showing, for example, what is wrong with Spencer's arguments that we should exclude grammar and history from the early years, and why Latin might be more valuable than more "useful" activities that have displaced it, and what are some major implications of his influential criterion of utility in constructing the curriculum. But I'll begin by demonstrating what is wrong with a principle that pretty well everyone thinks *is* wrong—that of recapitulation; showing how Spencer got even a good idea wrong and wrecked its potential value for a century and a half.

Recapitulation Again

Spencer was vague about how recapitulation was supposed to work. He assumed that because we can see an order in how the human race had gradually acquired various kinds of knowledge, "there will arise in every child an aptitude to acquire these kinds of knowledge in the same order" (1928, 61). Why? Well, that's where he becomes vague. Part of his answer is that "the race" and the child both follow that path from simple to complex, concrete to abstract, and so on. The other, connected part is that, faced with the phenomena of the world and trying to sort them out, "savages" and children in their minds will form similar impressions and responses to those impressions.

We have seen why this recapitulation principle was generally discarded, but it merits a closer look. Spencer wrecks his argument by focusing on *the knowledge* that the race and the child acquired. One problem was that the "phenomena" that surrounded the "savage," unlike those surrounding the modern child, did not include houses, streets, and carriages, and the language the "savage" heard in youth did not include theories about planets and stars, nor discussions of economics, nor expositions of laws of motion, heat, and so on. That is, the cognitive universe of the modern child is quite unlike that of Spencer's "savages."

We should reject Spencer's knowledge-based notion of recapitulation for the further reason that it doesn't allow us to design a sensible curriculum for modern students. One cannot sensibly teach about the stars, for example, by beginning with the "simple" views of "savages" and gradually elaborating them in the direction of modern cosmology. It would mean beginning with something like astrology, then giving accounts in which the sun orbits the earth, then reversing those accounts, and so forth.

Grammar

Let me now try to persuade you that Spencer was wrong in arguing that we should abolish the "intensely stupid" practice of teaching grammar to young children. He believed that its abstractness made it impossible for them, and its absence from most elementary schools today continues to be justified on similar grounds, even though Piaget is more commonly cited as a source of authority than Spencer.

I have already given reasons for disregarding Spencer's concrete-to-abstract principle, which formed one basis for the dismissal of grammar. In addition to Spencer's arguments, and no doubt deriving from them in part, a body of research studies since early in the twentieth century has accumulated in support of the claim that grammatical instruction leads to improvements in neither children's writing nor their comprehension. Worse, most children younger than fourteen seem to be confused by grammatical labels and distinctions among terms. (Find three auxiliary verbs on this page.) Such support, and the continuing belief in grammar's anti-utility in early years, means that an argument in its favor faces an uphill struggle. But here we go:

Grammar is our best description of the rules by which a language works. There are many ways of making these rules explicit and accessible to children. The beginnings of grammatical understanding come with a recognition that language does work according to rules, and children can begin to reflect on these rules almost as soon as they begin to speak.

Some of the more sophisticated models of how children learn language emphasize the importance of their becoming aware of language as an object on which they can reflect. In the process of acquiring language, children use "abstractions—not copies—of the linguistic input" (Karmiloff-Smith 1992, 51) and constantly re-describe and re-represent to themselves the nature of the language they use. Annette Karmiloff-Smith emphasizes that "the linguistic representations [that children form] themselves also undergo subsequent redescription, such that they become linguistic objects of attention outside their on-line use in comprehension and production. In other words, young children go beyond behavioral mastery, beyond fluent output and successful communication, to exploit the linguistic knowledge they have already stored. It is this that ultimately allows them to become little linguists" (48).

It has, relatedly, become increasingly clear that "encouragement of children's awareness of language structure and function will contribute to the emergence of literacy" (Herriman 1986, 159). What is commonly called "metalinguistic awareness" is recognized as tied to greater flexibility and competence in language-use and literacy. Courtney Cazden defines metalinguistic awareness as "the ability to make language forms opaque and attend to them in and for themselves" (1975, 63).

Early grammar study, then, can begin—as I recommend elsewhere (Egan 1988)—with the kind of jokes that draw attention to language as an object with peculiar and quite fascinating characteristics. ("What's a football made of?" "Pig's hide." "Why should they hide?" "No. The pig's outside." "Well bring him in. Any friend of yours is a friend of mine." Sorry 'bout that.) It is also an object whose peculiarities offer endless possibilities for fun. The temptation here (having piled up on my desk half a dozen joke books and wasted an hour flipping through them) is to fill a few pages with examples. While this would certainly lighten your reading load, I must reluctantly conclude that you are only too familiar with examples of jokes that rely on wordplay, drawing attention to language. We can go from "Teacher: 'Order!' Sarah: 'I'll have a hamburger and fries, please,'" to Lewis Carroll's curriculum of Reeling and Writhing, with Ambition, Distraction, Uglification, and Derision in Math class, along with Mystery, ancient and modern, and Fine Arts activities such as Drawling, Stretching, and Fainting in Coils, with, of course, the classics, Laughing and Grief.

But that's not grammar, you might object. That doesn't address what Spencer was trying to stop—the teaching of grammatical rules in the abstract and dry way they are laid out in textbooks. Spencer's argument was that children, in their early years, could understand language not as an object but only as a behavior. I am pointing casually to the fact that he was wrong—that children can readily perceive language as an abstract, rule-ordered object. (Jokes are mostly about the rules of language and what happens when you try to subvert them, ignore them, or deliberately misunderstand them.) Further, I am pointing out that children's ability to use language flexibly seems tied to their conscious understanding of its rules. The methods we choose to teach grammar, whether through jokes or lists of rules, is a separate question. No doubt we could agree that the methods Spencer deprecated usually induce boredom, but he gave reasons to dispense with teaching grammar altogether. Confusing methods of teaching with the educational value of grammar, he helped persuade generations of educationalists and teachers that they should ignore grammar, and so helped to produce generations of children who are linguistically less competent than they could and should be. The general perception that students are increasingly less linguistically able has encouraged some jurisdictions to reintroduce grammar teaching. Commonly it follows the old form that Spencer criticized and will no doubt spur a further Spencerian progressivist reaction against it—and properly so. The better trick, as I have argued (1997), is not to veer continually between these old alternatives but to work out how grammar can be made accessible, meaningful, and engaging to children who deploy particular sets of cognitive tools.

History

How about history's place in the Spencerian curriculum? He considered the history taught during his time as an accumulation of idle, inert facts, of no practical use for any of the main purposes of life. Many people felt that Spencer went too far in his dismissal and that he failed to recognize, as one contemporary put it, that history had a utility rather like travel: it "widens the student's mental vision, frees him to some extent from the bondage of the present, and prevents his mistaking conventionalities for laws of nature"

(Quick 1890, 448). This kind of conventional justification for including narrative history in the curriculum has its own problems, but because it is so commonly accepted today that some knowledge of the usual narratives of political and social history are important, I won't bother countering Spencer's general arguments here.

I do want to expose, however, a difficulty Spencer gets into when he recommends a "natural history of society" for the curriculum. Remember Beatrice Webb's comment that Spencer "looked on social institutions exactly as if they were plants or animals," and so the history he is willing to allow is a kind of sociology influenced by biology, which has become our modern social studies. Now recall also Spencer's guiding principle that "a child's intellectual instincts are more trustworthy than our reasonings" and that the ultimate criterion of worth is whether a curriculum topic induces "pleasurable excitement in the pupils" (1928, 63).

What is an educational theorist with these convictions to do when children show a marked preference for narrative history, dealing with personalities, conquests, heroism, the exotic, drama, and so on? And, adding insult to injury, when they show distaste for the "natural history of society"? (In nearly all surveys in recent decades, remember, social studies scores lowest or close to the lowest in students' interest.) Spencer concludes that children's common preference for the old-style narratives is "no proof of their worth" (1928, 27).

Having adopted many of the same ideas, John Dewey found himself in the same dilemma. He, too, declared that the history curriculum must focus on present social concerns: "A knowledge of the past and its heritage is of great significance when it enters into the present, but not otherwise" (1966, 75). How does some history, but not other, enter into the present? Well, because "it is important that education . . . use a criterion of social worth" (191), then "economic history is more human, more democratic, and hence more liberalizing than political history" (215–216). When children showed little interest in liberalizing economic history and much more interest in the heroic activities and vivid personalities of political history, Dewey's response was much the same as Spencer's. The theorists' child-centeredness extended only to the threshold of their different ideological convictions. When children's pleasure conflicts with the theorists' convictions, so much the worse for pleasure.

The main competitor to history for our minds' construction of the past is myth. As we reduce exposure to, and understanding of, history we increase the scope for myth. Past assessments of young children's understanding of history suggested that they had severe difficulties with the subject. Piaget's theory was taken as helping to explain why history was so hard for the young. This approach to the problem was vividly exemplified in Roy Hallam's Piagetian research project, which purported to show that students could not properly understand the "formal operational" concepts on which historical understanding relied until they reached age fourteen or fifteen (Hallam 1969).

History thus became considered "developmentally inappropriate" for younger children and the subject was largely removed from the primary years of schooling. Similar arguments are used today to defend social studies when some people suggest reintroducing history to the early years in its place. These arguments, which have effectively reduced the presence of history in the curriculum, have the same flaw that supports the exclusion of grammar. The subject was typically taught in a manner that tended to ignore the cognitive tools that children had in place to access it meaningfully. Having failed to use those means of access successfully, theorists claimed that the problem lay in the subject matter. The trick, again, is to attend to the cognitive tools children possess and teach understanding of history as one of the most important defenses against (the current epidemics of) provincialism and myth.

Latin and Useless Arts

Are you ready for Latin now? It has been a commonplace of progressivist educational theorizing that the presence of Latin in the curriculum was the clearest index of how education was out of tune with the needs of society. Spencer derided the classics in a style repeated endlessly through the twentieth century. He likened its use by the educated classes of his time to the tattoos and colored beads worn by "savages" (1928, 2), as merely a marker of status. When Latin or Greek is mentioned today, you may hear similar derisive comments from North American educationalists. The classics appear in the curricula of some exclusive private schools so that those children can grow up and trade Latin quips behind the backs of honest burghers at cocktail parties in order to make the Latin-less feel inferior, it seems.

Classical languages and literature have pretty well disappeared from the experience of North American children. They disappeared in response to the application of utilitarian principles to the curriculum and to the belief that learning them adequately is very difficult, so success in these languages marks off "elite" learners from the rest. (Or, at least, this is the case when they are taught as unimaginatively as was common.) Also, in modern multicultural societies, Latin and Greek would face competing claims from many other non-Western classical languages and literatures. A major agent in eradicating Latin from the curriculum was the foolish claim by its defenders early in the twentieth century—desperately responding to utilitarian pressures—that it did have the utility of making other subjects easier to learn and improved students' general intelligence. When Edward L. Thorndike ran some fairly mindless experiments in the early 1920s that purported to disprove these claims, Latin was helpless against the tough voices demanding that schools teach useful things to children.

The arguments for teaching Latin are that it, incidentally, assists that "metalinguistic awareness," mentioned above, in spades and, more important, that it provides access to reading Horace and company in other than more or less inadequate translations. How do we now compare the competing claims of Latin and a computer language for limited curriculum time? No contest. You would be in danger of being considered a tad demented for even suggesting the comparison. Those who learn a computer language well can look forward to a lucrative future and to serving a valuable social need. Those who learn Latin well, . . . well, they can read Horace in their spare time.

(In the nineteenth century, the British seem to have assumed that the classics provided an adequate training to run an empire. It was a training that allowed Sir Charles Napier when he conquered Sind to send back to London the single word message "Peccavi," confident that the administrators and politicians would get both the joke and the message. Peccavi = "I have sinned" [Sind].)

The makers of modern curricula have clearly concluded that Latin is an educational dinosaur—a fossil of something that once lived but lives no more. Its progress from prominence to near invisibility is one measure of the success of moving the new schools toward becoming utilitarian socializing institutions. I am using Latin as a vivid stand-in for all the "useless" subjects in the curriculum. If we are looking for winners in the competition for curriculum space, familiarization with spreadsheets and word-processing programs on a computer trumps familiarization with medieval history. Mathematics for household finance trumps algebra. (Horace Mann, 1796–1859, "the father of American public education," noted the absurdity of teaching all children algebra when hardly any of them would ever use it after their schooldays.)

But, you might reasonably respond, there is room for utilitarian subjects as well as art, Shakespeare, medieval history, and even, for those with a taste for it, Latin. The problem is that "useful" subjects have elbowed, and will continue to elbow, the "useless" from the curriculum. Each time some new utility arises—such as, recently, familiarization with computers—it can find curriculum space only by elbowing out, a bit further, the arts, Shakespeare, Latin, medieval history, and so on. Computing skills do not find curriculum space by elbowing out other useful subjects. So schools are pressured to buy more computers and have to buy less of something else, and it is usually library books—literature of the kind Spencer didn't have the time for—or musical instruments, or new history texts. This, anyway, is the current trend only too visible in my local schools. When push comes to shove in educational systems where a utilitarian criterion is dominant, humanity is diminished. Latin, art, and Shakespeare and company survive only because the utilitarian criterion has not absolutely pushed out criteria derived from academic ideals or from notions of individual development.

What is wrong is that the classics largely disappeared from the curriculum, and other "useless" arts are being diminished, on the basis of a principle that pays undue attention to one aspect of education and too little to others. I am suggesting not that we banish the useful from the curriculum but, rather, that we recognize that adopting Spencer's principles leaves us with inadequate defenses against the demands of utility.

The defense of Latin and the "useless" arts in the curriculum will have to be given in terms of the cultural-cognitive tools they provide. (See, for example, Kozulin's Vygotskian argument for Shakespeare as a cognitive "supertool"; 1998, ch. 6.)

The School and Social and Personal Goods

I wish to mention in passing why the kinds of schools we have, heavily committed to principles of utility while still adhering to principles of academic and personal development, have trouble achieving what have become their primary social purposes. The history of the curriculum since Spencer's time is largely an account of the consistent increase in activities that seem useful for "complete living" at the expense of traditional intellectual education. The trouble is that schools can be quite good institutions when they concentrate sensibly on intellectual education, but they are less good at developing the whole person or producing good citizens or ensuring parenting skills or generally equipping children with the main items on Spencer's list of priorities.

Why is the school not good at doing what Spencer concluded are the most important preparations for adult life? Well, groups of about thirty children in the charge of a single adult are not an ideal format for training in "life skills." As John Locke observed rather caustically, "The principles of justice, generosity, and sobriety, joined with observation and industry, [are] qualities which I judge school boys do not learn much from one another" (1964, 52). Unless the school has enormous power and authority over children, which in a democracy we are unwilling to allow, the dominant values and behavioral norms will be those the children bring to the school and against which any competing values and norms of the teachers' will be largely helpless. I realize that many teachers would not accept such a claim. Indeed, one who read the draft of this book on my Website protested that most teachers are good at keeping renegades under control and creating conditions of good, civil order in classrooms. But even so, the virtues of good democratic citizenship cannot adequately be learned—as Spencer might have pointed out—by rules, nor can they be well modeled by an institution that cannot be organized or run democratically.

The teachers of democratic virtues are the family and society. In comparison with the lessons they teach, for better or worse, the school's influence, along with its social studies classes, is close to negligible. The fact that so many families might be dysfunctional and the society most children encounter might not ideally exemplify democratic virtues doesn't make the school a good place to compensate for them. Having generally accepted Spencer's criteria, however, the school has been defenseless against becoming a dumping ground for all of society's problems with the young. That so many problems the young face today are urgent and desperate still doesn't make the school an adequate institution to deal with them, but in trying to deal with them, however ineffectually, schools guarantee that they will not accomplish the traditional academic job adequately either.

Locke made the further point that "virtue is harder to be got than a knowledge of the world" (1964, 49). Virtue may be more important than knowledge of the world, but the school is not much good at teaching virtue. It can, however, make a go of teaching knowledge of the world. This is too simple a contrast, of course. But the great pressures on schools to do the socializing job that Spencer's principles have encouraged consistently undermines their ability to produce, say, the academic "excellence" others also require of them.

Knowledge in Places Other Than the Mind

In general, Spencer argued that we should not stuff children's minds with useless knowledge. It is easier to agree with this generalization than to work out what knowledge is useless or what makes some knowledge useful for some at some times and useless for them or for others at other times. I can still recall (on a good day) provisions of the Treaties of Augsburg and Nanking. Is the Treaty of Nanking more useful and valuable than the Treaty of Augsburg because it might help me to understand China's stance toward the West today? Are those facts, and the rest of my knowledge, simply inert and useless until I can find a pragmatic use for them? And if that is the case, would I be better off not stuffing my inadequate brain with lots of facts, memorized speeches and poems, formulas and stories, and so on, but rather focusing attention on how to acquire knowledge when I need it? Or, as a subheadline to a column in my local paper put it: "The knowledge explosion means no student can ever learn enough. The ability to find where it is stored is essential." The headline was: "Back-to-Basics Learning at Odds with Computer Age." The columnist wrote, "If I had to make a choice, I'd much rather have a child who knew where things were than what they were—beyond, obviously, a certain basic level."

What is wrong with this descendant of Spencer's principle is that it pays too little attention to how the mind uses knowledge. The provisions of the Treaty of Nanking and that sonnet of Shakespeare that you learned by heart do not exist in the mind as in a library. The mind is an organ that perceives and feels as well as knows, and the three, along with other features of our mental lives, are combined in ways we haven't the vaguest understanding of. What we know forms a resource for our imaginations. All the facts in the library that I know how to locate do not inform the way my imagination works. All the poems stored on a computer will influence the rhythms of our language and our images and emotions not a whit, whereas those we learned by rote are a constant resource for the imagination when we write or talk or lie silent in the night.

As I suggested in the previous chapter, the curriculum through the twentieth century increasingly focused on "skills" and decreasingly on rote learning. The very term *rote learning,* denoting a kind of learning that is supposed to be pointless and meaningless, has displaced the hard practice of having students learn by heart. Spencer's influence has impoverished the imaginations of generations of students.

And again, of course, to view as competitors knowing things and knowing where to find things is, like many of the mutually exclusive alternatives we are offered in education, a bit daft. The more you know, the more you discover where to find what you don't know.

The mind is not a zero-sum container. Indeed, paradoxically, it seems closer to the opposite: the more you know, the more you can learn.

So the fact that Spencer acutely diagnosed the problem that students were accumulating inert knowledge does not justify his solutions to the problem.

. . . .

INTO THE TWENTIETH CENTURY

Perhaps the most directly and extensively influential document about education in North America was the 1918 report of the Commission on the Reorganization of Secondary Education. Lawrence Cremin wrote that "most of the important and influential movements in the field since 1918 have simply been footnotes to the classic itself" (1955, 307). And a standard curriculum textbook declares: "Its impact on educational policy has yet to be equaled" (Tanner and Tanner 1980, 275). The committee that produced the report was appointed by the National Education Association in 1913 and, it is fair to say, labored long and hard to convert a number of Spencer's curriculum principles into a form that fitted the American context. The report declared that the purpose of education was "to prepare for the duties of life." The cardinal principles it enunciated were to form the criteria that determine the curriculum: health, command of fundamental processes, worthy home membership, vocation, citizenship, worthy use of leisure, and ethical character. Knowledge that would support these principles was the knowledge of most worth. Spencer would no doubt have felt satisfied that his message had crossed the Atlantic without significant distortion.

As I have indicated, Spencer's influence met greater resistance in his home country than in North America. The main prominent and influential resister was Sir Robert Morant, the first secretary of the new Board of Education for England and Wales, created in the

year of Spencer's death, 1902. Morant oversaw the development of
the new state secondary education system basing it on the British
"public" (that is, with exquisite logic, private) schools, with a prior-
ity given to traditional humanistic studies and little emphasis on
science and technology. Some have argued that Morant bears some
responsibility for Britain's relative economic decline through the
twentieth century because he established educational priorities
that paid inadequate attention to the skills most needed for economic development during that period. Others, of course, praise
him for standing for civilized values against crude utility. (Yet others think that school curricula have only the remotest influence on
the economic fortunes of states.) While in the United States, the
report of the Commission on Reorganization of Secondary Education was a progressive document aimed at increasing social efficiency, the British Fisher Act of the same time included such sentiments about those to whom educational provision was to be
extended as: "They want [education] because they know that in the
treasures of the mind they can find aid to good citizenship, a source
of pure enjoyment and refuge from the necessary hardships of life
spent in the midst of clanging machinery in our hideous cities of
toil."

But even Britain could not resist the demands of utility. The desire to fashion some schools as more effective instruments of the
economy and social welfare led to the creation of the distinctive
Central Schools in the 1930s as a result of the W. H. Tawney–influenced Hadow Report. This report contained the interesting observation that "many people feel ill at ease in an atmosphere of books and
lessons," and schooling for such people should of course be designed
to spare them this discomfort. The 1931 *Report of the Consultative
Committee on the Primary School* in Britain saw the further injection
of Spencerian ideas. The report's authors emphasized the need to get
away from "subjects" and work much harder at "relating the curricu-

lum more closely to the natural movement of the children's minds" (xix). Teachers were to substitute for their traditional practice the new "methods which take as the starting-point of the work of the primary school the experience, the curiosity, and the awakening powers of the children themselves" (xx). In another echo of Spencer, the report's authors concluded that "the curriculum should not be loaded with inert ideas and crude blocks of facts" and that crucial for young children's learning is greater "concreteness" (xx).

The experience of the Great Depression through the 1930s in the United States led to calls for greater "relevance" in schools' curricula—relevance, that is, to the needs of a faltering economy and to the better vocational preparation of students. The story for the rest of the century is not significantly different. Whether in the 1940 report from the American Council of Education ("What the High Schools Ought to Teach") or the 1944 report on "Education for ALL Americans" or the British 1944 Education Act resulting from the Spens and Horwood report, increasing emphasis was laid on the schools' responsibility to produce practical competence for citizenship and adequate preparation for jobs. Refined academic training was preserved as a luxury for the few, while socializing activities were the pragmatic requirements for the many.

The secondary school was made a more effective agent of social utility by decoupling it from college and university programs. Energetic arguments were persuasive in increasing the secondary curriculum's autonomy from preparation for "higher" academic pursuits most students would never engage in. The "Eight Year Study" was one of its effective supports (Giles et al. 1942). This decoupling has still not gone as far as some would wish but, during the middle decades of the century, it went sufficiently far for the high school experience to increasingly emphasize preparation for work and citizenship rather than preparation for college and scholarly pursuits. Some disillusion with the results of this "useful" move has led some

North American school districts to retreat toward a slightly more academic curriculum.

The growing influence of the criterion of utility to social and economic ends has also generated a disjunction between the secondary and primary school. The utilitarian criterion can work efficiently for the secondary years, when students are being prepared with the range of particular skills required for their planned social and economic roles. But the utilitarian criterion is much less efficient for the primary years, when the urgencies of vocational training and future citizenship commitments and college courses that lead to professional qualifications are more remote and diluted. The tough voices that speak on behalf of utility today attend to the primary years only when it becomes obvious that inefficiencies there are compromising the secondary training programs. Then we get "back to basics" movements. But as long as students are delivered to the secondary schools with functional literacy and numeracy, then there are no compelling utilitarian pressures on the curriculum of early schooling. The result has tended to be primary school curricula and practices that encourage experiment and play and secondary curricula and practices that emphasize attainment of clear standards in tightly organized subjects.

· ·

SPENCER'S INFLUENCE ON DEWEY

Occasionally a textbook about the history of education in the United States shows a recognition that "Spencer ranks as one of the great pioneers of American progressivism. He underscored the tenets of progressive education so forcefully that he anticipated much of the work of John Dewey" (Rippa 1997, 148). Given Dewey's continuing and apparently increasing influence among professional educationalists in North America, it seems worth briefly underlining how strongly the fundamental principles of his work repeat ideas articulated by Spencer.

Dewey accepts Spencer's starting principle that "the curriculum must be planned with reference to placing essentials first, and refinements second," and that the "subject matter of education consists primarily of the meanings which supply content to existing social life" (Dewey 1966, 191, 192). He shares Spencer's hostility to and contempt for the "ornamental" curriculum that was supposed to have been the fare of classically educated elites.

We have seen that Dewey shared Spencer's view of the kind of history that was to be avoided. He favored economic, industrial, and intellectual history because they demonstrate to the child the "successive causes of social progress" and "make plain how the entire advance of humanity from savagery to civilization has been dependent on intellectual discoveries and inventions" (1966, 215, 217). Traditional history both considered sterile, and Dewey supports Spencer's view that the only proper use of history is as "an organ for analysis of the warp and woof of the present social fabric" (217).

Echoing Spencer again, Dewey declares education to be properly not an "affair of 'telling' and being told, but an active and constructive process" (1966, 38). He thus supports Spencer's view that each topic should have a "purely experimental" introduction. Dewey's way of putting it is that students must always be involved in "an actual empirical situation as the initiating phase of thought" (153). Both theorists connect this conclusion with their arguments for the importance of science in the curriculum. Dewey's only reference to Spencer in *Democracy and Education*, originally published in 1916, is the marginally libelous claim that Spencer believed "that scientific knowledge could be communicated in ready-made form" (221). The margin that is not quite libelous is due to Spencer's not having discussed explicitly how children were to be introduced to the methods of science—though there are surely enough statements and illustrations in his work to make it clear that he did not expect children to begin learning science other than experimentally. Dewey's Spencerian belief that "learning in school should be continuous with that out of school" (358), tied to the two men's shared view of experimental beginnings for science study, suggest that the practical consequences of Dewey's ideas would be indistinguishable from what would follow from Spencer's.

We looked also at Spencer's hostility to "forcing" and precociousness as against nature and the implications of such ideas for the curriculum. Dewey similarly claimed that "we violate the child's nature and render difficult the best ethical results by introducing the child too abruptly to a number of special studies, of reading, writing, geography, etc. out of relation with social life" (1964, 432). This belief that the child's nature can inform us about when to introduce topics has received further support in the theories of Piaget. One result has been the increasing reduction through the twentieth century of the academic content available in primary classrooms.

Perhaps I should emphasize this point, for it seems not much commented on. Spencer, Dewey, and Piaget all argued for reducing, simplifying, and "concretizing" the curriculum for young children. A consequence of this trivializing of the primary curriculum is that children do not learn the prerequisites to later learning, and this trivialization that begins in the early years has an impoverishing effect on students' abilities to learn throughout their schooling. For example, the flawed arguments that led to the removal of history from the primary curriculum and its displacement by social studies has, as a consequence, students' later reduced ability to understand history.

It would be easy to fill pages with Dewey's echoes of Spencer, despite Dewey's socialism and Spencer's "social Darwinism." Both reacted strongly against traditional forms of education, which they saw—as did Locke and Rousseau, and Plato and pretty well all educational reformers—as a desiccated mass of subject matter that was "remote and dead—abstract and bookish" (Dewey 1966, 8). They believed that they better understood the nature of the child than did traditional educators and recognized that much of the curriculum content taught to children remained inert, because either, or both, the method or time of teaching violated the child's nature. They knew this because they also knew that learning was natural and pleasurable, and if children were failing to learn or learning with difficulty and pressure, the cause lay in the curriculum or in the methods or time of teaching. If most children were failing to learn certain curriculum material adequately, it then followed that this material should either be delayed until they were "ready" to learn it or be ditched from the curriculum as, anyway, ornamental and useless. Neither Spencer or Dewey was in any way hostile to the attainment of academic excellence, but both emphasized that one could not begin with academic subject-matter and expect the child to make sense of it. As Dewey wrote, in words that could have been Spencer's: "Hence the first approach to any subject in school, if thought is to be aroused and not words acquired, should be as unscholastic as possible. To realize what an experience, or empirical situation, means, we have to call to mind the sort of situation that presents itself outside of school; the sort of occupations that interest and engage activity in ordinary life" (1966, 154).

Their diagnosis of why formal education seems to be relatively ineffective has found very general agreement. It will be ineffective when the nature of the learner is largely ignored, when the curriculum is irrelevant to children's experience, when current social life does not inform the school's activities, and so on. These ideas are usually associated with "progressivism" because they were early and most vigorously articulated by people who allied themselves with that movement. But it is important to recognize that most of these ideas have now become common presuppositions of very many in education who would not consider themselves progressivists.

It seems too obvious to require much demonstration that the radical writers on education during the 1960s were repeating Spencer's principles again—though commonly citing Dewey as their source. Let me take a single example almost at random, showing how Spencer's extreme claim that following the promptings of nature would allow us to do away with having to specify a curriculum altogether. The "deschooling" movement was based on this principle, but we can see it also at use by those who wanted a radical reform of the curriculum. Neil Postman and Charles Weingartner wrote an essay with the updated Spencerian title "What's Worth Knowing?" (1969, 161–176). They ask their readers to imagine a world in which all the textbooks have vanished, creating the "opportunity to increase the relevance of schools" (162). Instead of the currently irrelevant curriculum they propose a means of generating one from the questions that the children themselves raise. Such a procedure, they tell us in Spencerian terms, will ensure that "the student is not a passive 'recipient'; he becomes an active *producer* of knowledge" (164). Examples of crucial questions run through the set of issues that Spencer listed as the most important things in life from which the curriculum was to begin. They confidently declare that their questions-curriculum "is based on what we know about learners, and not on what we know about what we want them to learn" (171). Traditional curricula and the standards of achievement they require *"do not exist in natural, human learning situations"* (168, emphasis in original). It could have been Spencer; it was.

In the old battle between rhetoric and philosophy, Spencer struck a doughty blow on behalf of rhetoric. To the degree that his ideas were influential on those who were organizing the new schools for all children, they became institutions to train for the programmatic tasks of life and, given the twentieth-century world of competing nations, to equip populations with the skills to drive national progress. Spencer argued loudly that the British "public" schools of his time were a distinct hindrance to national progress. Had he lived, he would have predicted that Sir Robert Morant's preservation of traditional liberal educational principles would have contributed to Britain's relative economic decline through the twentieth century. And he would have predicted that the progressive principles that made greater headway in the United States would have contributed to its relative economic success.

Those a little less precipitous than Spencer in recognizing large-scale cause-and-effect relations between educational methods and the civic and economic health of a nation wonder how useful educational methods are to national success. In the United States, comparisons with school performance in other countries are frequent, and "stakeholders" in schools are alert to differences between those in the United States and those of their major economic competitors. During the 1980s, for example, many politicians and business groups called for an increase in the time children spent in school, because Japan's superior economic growth was assumed to be caused in significant degree by the greater number of hours Japanese children spent on school tasks. That East German children also spent more hours in school seemed not to be considered relevant. During the period of rising crime statistics, calls were made for improving the teaching of civic virtues in schools. It would be a brave person who would try to tie the decline in crime statistics through the 1990s to some change in social studies teaching during the period. Some have credited altered policing techniques, but the reduction in crime statistics occurred also in jurisdictions without newer policing techniques. And yet braver people have pointed to the increased availability of abortion fifteen or twenty years earlier than the improvement in crime statistics.

I am reminded of Anthony Burgess's fictionalized Sigmund Freud (in *The End of the World News*) who is being interrogated by Nazi officials. Freud complains how the country is being undermined by the machinations of the cyclists. The Nazis are puzzled. "Why the cyclists?" Freud replies, "Why the Jews?"

What I am trying to point out is the very considerable difficulty of tying educational cause to social effect. What I think we can do is tie educational cause to educational effect, and it is the educational ideas of progressivism and their less than wonderful educational effects that I am trying to tie together.

Spencer and Dewey have been properly celebrated for diagnosing a central problem of formal education: that students can learn a great deal about the world and yet remain bored and unable to use the knowledge to enrich their experience. That knowledge can remain "inert" is indeed a central practical problem of education. Those who are technically minded study the nature of learning or development as though there are mysteries about these processes whose solution will enable teachers to become much more efficient and will allow us to design more efficient curricula. Spencer presented both a diagnosis and a solution to the problem of inertness. Dewey largely repeated both, at greater length, in his own inimitable (one hopes) style. We have had a century or more of attempts to make their solution work. Either it is extraordinarily difficult (which they and their followers assure us is the opposite of the case), or teachers are generally so stupid that they can't manage to follow their prescriptions, or there is something wrong with their solution. I have argued that the last of these alternatives is the explanation. Apart from the ideas about learning and development Spencer bequeathed us, the curriculum that has been increasingly shaped by the influence of Spencer's ideas has not delivered anything like what was, and is constantly, promised.

What the increase in utility has delivered are an impoverished curriculum and an unforgivable ignorance. Instead of solving the problem of how to make inert knowledge live in students' experience, the criterion of utility has dealt with the problem by declaring that the inert knowledge is irrelevant to students' experience (which is proved by its being inert) and so should be removed from the curriculum. The subprinciple that only knowledge that is used will be remembered and be meaningful to students has reduced the role of the arts, humanities, and history in students' experience. We use the word *catastrophe* now for any kind of disaster, but it derives from Greek drama and its special force characterizes disasters that did not need to occur and are brought about by our own flawed intentions. The intentions may be noble and for the best, but the flaw inexorably leads to catastrophe. I think the word is properly used about our schools and the principles Herbert Spencer so persuasively articulated.

No doubt I am guilty of the simplistic cause-and-effect connecting I complained about just above. But I do think twentieth-century education was haunted by the wrong solution to the problem of inertness. The trick is to work out how to make "inert" knowledge live — not give up and declare knowledge to be "irrelevant" to students' experience. What kind of impoverishment of experience are we happy to accept in such a claim? In weaseling out of the problem this way we have created an anemic curriculum significantly handed over to anemic socialization.

chapter 5

· ·

RESEARCH HAS

· ·

SHOWN THAT . . .

· ·

I would like to persuade you now that the commonly used phrase that is this chapter's title is rarely justified in education. I shall give reasons to believe that what are currently considered the most rigorous and reliable forms of research yield results that are less secure than is commonly believed; that other largely ignored forms can be more secure; and that the insecurity of the so-called reliable research is tied up with the flaw I have identified in progressivism and the security of the largely ignored research is tied up with those cognitive tools I have been alluding to. In a sermon in his hometown in 1427, Saint Bernardino of Siena noted that a "preacher must approach a delicate subject as a rooster walks on dung: by stepping carefully" (Polecritti 2000). The same is true for the writer on education when approaching dangerous territory. Perhaps I might try to step carefully by describing a personal dilemma.

Some years ago, shortly after the Punic Wars, I suggested that we could take some of the elements that make stories so engaging to children and use them in shaping lessons in mathematics, science, language arts, and so on (Egan 1979). I didn't mean that we should tell fictional stories about the educational material but rather that we should organize the educational material into forms that had story characteristics. I designed a framework to help plan lessons and units to do this, with a variety of examples (Egan 1986), and was delighted when teachers here and there said they found the framework made their planning and teaching more interesting and improved their students' learning and engagement with the material.

Teachers and curriculum coordinators occasionally contacted me, saying they were trying to organize workshops or projects to introduce the framework to others, but more senior administrators were unwilling to authorize such activities until they were informed of the "research base" for the procedures specified in the framework. Supporters of the story-form framework seemed disappointed when I told them that there was no "research base"; it was simply my attempt to systematize some common features of the best teaching practice I had witnessed over the years and to provide some theoretical support for it. That there might be theoretical support was taken as quite irrelevant; results of empirical testing were what the administrators required.

To respond to the reasonable questions about whether use of the framework achieved in practice what I suggested it would, I applied for research funding and was lucky to get support that extended, with extensions, over six years. With the help of research assistants and some generous colleagues, we ran a number of studies—qualitative, quantitative, focus-group discussions, and so on. The results? Tons of data, bulging files, a stack of tapes, and, in me, some bewilderment. Did the model work? Well, of course it did. So where are the published reports of the research—the "research base" that administrators wanted?

The data—the files and tapes—sit here, and I haven't been able to bring myself to write it up. Why not? Well, that is in part what I want to explore, in a less personal way, in this chapter. I couldn't persuade myself that all the research efforts over the six years actually showed anything reliably generalizable that wasn't logically entailed by the arguments I had made at the beginning. Now that rather packed sentence is what I want to unfurl and justify, not just for my case but for much empirical research in education.

My dilemma was that I could write up the research to show how use of the story-form framework had, after some training, had beneficial effects on students' learning, as well as on the teachers who became familiar with it. There were the usual variations among the teachers and students, but none of the data made me any more or less confident about using the framework in primary classrooms. During these years I was also reading extensively in the history of educational research, and I was struck by the huge number of studies that had shown, like my small study, successful implementation of ideas, frameworks, programs, materials, techniques, teaching methods, and so on. Some were reports of massively funded studies, others were on a smaller scale, and still others were synthesizing analyses of sets of studies. Occasionally an article points to the failure of the experimental group to do as well as controls, but such results are relatively rare. By and large we have available a resource of gazillions of studies showing us how to improve students' learning at every grade level in every subject using an array of procedures and technologies.

A number of scholars have tried to explain why this torrent of educational research and its mass of findings seem to have had no discernible impact on general educational achievement. Another feature of the literature I had been immersed in is the consistent claim, made in much the same language since Herbert Spencer's time, that applying scientific methods to education will lead to a revolution in learning. The transformation that science has been consistently on the point of delivering still doesn't loom very large in statistics of student achievements today. And where one can see dramatic achievements, they seem to result rather from a charismatic teacher or administrator, and, it appears from reading many reports of such dramatic achievements, the methods of teaching, the materials, and the technologies involved in these improvements are enormously varied and seem quite secondary.

When I am imprudent enough to begin this line of argument with educational researcher colleagues, I am referred to professor x's large-scale, international project, which is showing significant improvements in students' achievements, or to professor y's project, also having exciting results, or to professor z's findings that promise a deeper understanding of the learning process itself, leading to new and powerful intervention strategies. To the researchers immersed in this work, major improvements, new strategies, and the expansion of our understanding of human intelligence, learning, and development are everywhere evident.

If I am really imprudent and say that these exemplary programs and exciting results have been the staple of educational research literature for three quarters of a century at least, I am told that the new research paradigms and expanding knowledge of neurophysiology, expert performance, metacognition, or whatever, makes current research quite different from earlier narrow and confused work.

If I am blind drunk and persist, pointing out that those confused predecessors said all the same things about their predecessors and claimed that their new paradigm was in the throes of delivering the real benefits of science to education, . . . well, I just get myself into trouble. I am sometimes accused, perhaps accurately, of being incorrigibly ignorant about current research, and also of being antiscience. This second accusation, at least, is false. At issue is what the scientific study of education requires, and my argument is that those requirements are not being adequately met by most of the self-consciously "scientific" research in education today.

Now I don't wish to pretend, with the scenario of my story-form framework, that I was a committed educational researcher suddenly struck with doubts. I had, after all, published a book critical of research in education some time earlier—parts of which I draw on below (Egan 1983). That book grew out of a gradual disenchantment with the uses made of Piaget's theory in education. Early in what can only laughingly be called my career, I used to teach the introductory psychology of education course in my institution and, as a part of that course, to teach about Piaget's theory and its educational implications. As time passed, I became increasingly skeptical about the claimed implications of the theory and concerned about the practices promulgated in its name, and then skeptical about the theory itself, and then skeptical about pretty well the whole of the course material. A case of galloping skepticism or, as some of my researcher colleagues claim, of galloping brain-eating disease. The educational psychology of the day focused on topics, issues, and problems that increasingly seemed to me to be different, often in quite subtle ways, from what mattered in education. And I have read nothing of late to convince me that more recent empirical research in education has got a better grip on educational phenomena.

Medieval monarchs occasionally would have in their courts an official fool. The fool was licensed by the monarch's authority to say anything and be secure from punishment. King Lear's "all-licensed fool" is perhaps the best-known example in English literature of this historical peculiarity. Even the most despotic monarchs sometimes recognized the usefulness of having someone around who was licensed to say the otherwise unsayable. Perhaps cognitive science colleagues and other educational researchers might grant me a fool's license to say what is, if not unsayable, at least not much said, or, if much said, at least not much heard, about the status of their enterprise.

. . . .

BERNARDINO'S ROOSTER'S PARADIGM

The reason for stepping carefully, and the reason that delicacy is required, is not because there is something obviously wrong with the position I want to argue against. If it were obviously wrong, so many intelligent people, many of whose work I admire and draw on, would hardly continue to accept it. It is not the kind of thing one can amass a set of facts to disprove; the facts of educational research are not in dispute. It's rather the deep presuppositions on which the enterprise of the currently dominant forms of educational research rest that I want to call into question. It's more an angle of vision that I want to dispute, or perhaps it's a matter of paradigms—to draw warily on a much-abused term. In a paradigm shift, in Thomas Kuhn's classic account (1962), the facts are not in dispute; rather, what shifts is the way the facts are seen, the context of meaning within which their relations are established. What I am trying to suggest here is a way of looking at education and educational research that will move current forms of empirical research from their position as the scientific driving force that promises major improvements in education to an activity using suspect methods that mostly miss the educational point.

Constantly, from Spencer's time to the latest textbooks in educational psychology, the analogy is repeated that as physics is to engineering so psychology is to education or, in what seems to be the increasingly preferred version, as biology is to medicine so psychology is to education. The shift in paradigm, or angle of vision, I want to encourage you to try on, if only provisionally, sees these analogies as flawed and misleading. It is well to remember that in Kuhn's characterization, psychology is preparadigmatic in the strict sense in which he writes about scientific revolutions. Psychology, for all the talk of science and scientific research in education, is not a science like physics or biology. And education is unlike engineering in that education is value-saturated in ways that engineering is not. And education is unlike medicine in that although the general conception of "health" may be occasionally contested, medicine can provide the doctor with a largely unproblematic aim for intervention; such a relatively clear aim does not exist in the conceptual ferment of "education," where radically different ends and purposes are vividly contested.

The paradigm I want to shift you from is evident in the constant observation that children's learning is obviously a part of the natural world and consequently conforms to laws that we can set about discovering. The paradigm I want to have you try on is to see our learning as indeed a part of the natural world but to recognize that human nature is shaped by evolution, development, history, technology, and culture. To explore human learning using scientific methods derived from study of the physical world may prove too much of a stretch—a bridge too far, one might say.

The promise of new knowledge about how children learn is echoed constantly from Spencer's day to such recent claims as: "The working of the mind and the brain are now subject to powerful research tools. From that research a science of learning is emerging" (Donovan et al. 1999, 5). Now, although it would be easy to search out the more aggressive and assertive claims of, say, cognitive science's contributions to education, I don't wish to suggest that the position I am arguing against is one held only by people who have exaggerated notions of their grasp on the topics they are researching. To quote from a work related to that above: "what has been learned about the principles that guide some aspects of learning do not constitute a complete picture of the principles that govern all domains of learning. The scientific bases, while not superficial in themselves, do represent only a surface level of a complete understanding of the subject" (Bransford et al. 1999, 14). What I want you to envision is a paradigm in which "a complete understanding of the subject," even if that were attainable, would not help education in the way assumed. (And perhaps I need again to note that I recognize that many would consider my target here to constitute only one subarea of the discipline. But stick with me; the Gatling gun is on a swivel.)

The common argument made by those who have questioned what they call the scientific pretensions of the social sciences is that human behavior and culture are more complicated than physical phenomena and that applying to behavior and culture the methods that have proven so effective in dealing with the physical world does not get us a similar understanding of the human world. Having scientific methods, that is to say, is only half the battle; the methods have to be appropriate to the phenomena they are used on — and that's the half that causes us problems with regard to education. The most celebrated statement of the problem, referring to psychology, is: "The existence of the experimental method makes us think we have the means of solving the problems which trouble us; though problem and method pass one another by" (Wittgenstein 1963, 232).

Earlier Lev Vygotsky had made a similar observation: "A concept that is used deliberately, not blindly, in the science for which it was created, where it originated, developed and was carried to it ultimate expression, is *blind*, leads nowhere, when transposed to another science. Such blind transpositions, of the biogenetic principle, the experimental and mathematical method from the natural sciences, created the appearance of science in psychology which in reality concealed a total impotence in the face of studied facts" (1997, 280).

My main reason for urging some skepticism about claims in education that begin with this chapter's title may be seen as an elaboration of Wittgenstein's observation that the methods of research commonly pass by the educational problems we need to solve. He characterized the psychology of his day as suffering a defect that might also be directed at much current educational research: we see a combination of "experimental methods and *conceptual confusion*" (1963, 232; emphasis in original).

This general criticism might be ignored today as possibly having had some relevance to behaviorism but not to the new cognitive science that draws on rapidly advancing knowledge in developmental psychology, neuroscience, anthropology, cross-cultural research, and so on. "Today," as one of the most energetic projects aimed at designing programs based only on secured scientific findings about learning puts it, "the world is in the midst of an extraordinary outpouring of scientific work on the mind and brain, on the processes of thinking and learning, on neural processes that occur during thought and learning, and on the development of competence" (Bransford et al. 1999, 3). I am as excited as anyone about what this new knowledge exposes about the human mind, but I am skeptical of the old paradigm's assumption that this knowledge provides a significant resource to improve education.

Well, again I have mumbled on trying to articulate a particular position, only to realize that I am simply echoing in part positions better stated by others. In this case, I might have done a more convincing job by frequent reference to the work of Jerome Bruner, and particularly to the distinction he has made between paradigmatic and narrative forms of cognition, and the consequent differences in the modes of inquiry we should sensibly use for each (1986, 1990, 1996; see also Bakhurst and Shanker 2001).

. . . .

UNITS OF EDUCATION

Dealing with the odd question "What is a unit of education?" may help to catch for a moment the alternative angle of vision, or paradigm, I want to encourage. Though odd, it isn't a silly question for an educational researcher to address. After all, if the thing we are researching is not a unit of what we want to know about, then we shouldn't be surprised if our research yields knowledge that proves unhelpful in dealing with the problems that prompted it. My not-so-hidden agenda is to suggest that failure to identify units of education is one key to understanding why so much educational research seems to have had no discernible beneficial effects on education. What is at issue here, to repeat, are not facts but ways of seeing, and to help my argument, later I use a visual-based metaphor.

Now I don't wish to simplify to the point of confusion, but one of the keys to success for those methods of inquiry we unambiguously call sciences seems to have been connected with their ability to isolate appropriate units of their object of study—molecules, cells, atoms, and so on. Astronomy, for example, had been largely an amateur pursuit until means were devised to isolate and analyze light. Linguistics made rapid advances in the rigor with which it handles its subject matter since isolating analytically fruitful units— which turned out not to be letters, words, and sentences but rather phonemes, morphemes, and phrases. In the physical sciences, the units of study do not decompose into another level without qualitative changes occurring in appropriate methods of inquiry— molecular chemistry and subatomic physics adapt their methodologies to their basic units of study. And the morpheme, say, as an analytically fruitful linguistic unit does not decompose into the phoneme without different methods of analysis coming into play. (I recognize that I am putting this a tad simplistically.)

But in human events, our problems in identifying units are greater. "She walked into the rose garden" is some kind of unit of behavior, but it is one that readily decomposes into other units of behavior, such as "She pulled open the gate" and "She stepped down onto the gravel path." And these can be decomposed further and further, until one might reach a biological or physical science account. But none of the decomposed units would help us understand the initial unit in the way we want: What were her motives for entering the rose garden? What did she hope or fear? What were the implications of the event? That is, the meaning of "She entered the rose garden"—the thing that makes it a unit of behavior—seems to be determined by something beyond the event itself. If we know that her entering the rose garden is the event that brings some story to a climax, then we may be satisfied that we know its meaning as a part of a plot.

That is, an oddity of what we might identify as units of human behavior is that their unit-ness is determined by our knowing the larger unit of which they are a part. There are no natural units of human behavior, except on a purely physiological level, because what we count as a unit—an action or event—is determined by the larger frame of meanings in which it plays a part. (For an elaboration of this argument, see Egan 1978.)

How, then, are we to identify what are units of education? The implication of the above seems to be that we cannot know unless we know the larger frame of meanings that establishes anything as a unit of education. We can ensure that something is an educational unit only if we know how it plays a part in a conception of education, an educational theory. That is, without an educational theory, we lack the means for determining units of education.

Maybe this is beginning to seem arcane. Let me try to clarify it by introducing the metaphor that I hope will do some work for me. Think of the educated person as a complex image. We can think of this image in two ways. The first way is to see this person as made up of a large set of pieces, like a complex jigsaw puzzle, which are the knowledge, skills, attitudes, and so on to be learned until the student increasingly approximates in her or his own unique way a "family resemblance" of our image of the educated person. Teaching the causes of the American Civil War thus becomes an educational unit because an understanding of this event is a part of what we expect in an educated person.

The second way to see the image of education is as like a hologram. If the plate containing the interference pattern of the holographic image is broken into pieces, each piece contains an image of the whole; the smaller the piece, the more blurred the image that can be constituted by the laser's light; the larger the piece, the clearer the image. Teaching about the causes of the Civil War, in this case, will be an educational unit only if it is taught in a way that is infused by the conception of education that makes it an educational unit.

The work I want this metaphor to do is help show education as a process that is better represented by the second way of seeing our image of the educated person. The metaphor points up why some knowledge can be meaningless unless, like pieces of the holographic plate, it embodies an image of the whole of which it is a part. The two-dimensional picture may be broken into many clear and vivid pieces—a cloud, a tree, a boot, a smiling face, a blue eye, a battle scene—but if they individually hold no clue to the image of which they are parts, they will remain separate and inert.

The trouble is that standing still with one eye closed in front of a holographic image prevents us distinguishing it from a two-dimensional picture. Perhaps I am pushing my metaphor too far here, but I want to suggest that much educational research is guided by psychological theories and not educational ones. How can one tell the difference when it comes to considering educational research? If you have become accustomed to looking at educational phenomena through psychological rather than educational theories, it isn't so easy to tell. It's the conceptual equivalent of standing still with one eye closed in front of a hologram. Nothing that can be pointed at can show the difference. We require the paradigm shift of opening the other eye and moving.

Well, that's a rather self-righteous and pompous way of putting it, and that's why the metaphor begins to be less useful when pushed this far. But it does help us see why looking at education in a certain way might not bring out aspects of its phenomena that remain nevertheless hugely important and central to its distinctiveness.

Psychology, and to a lesser extent sociology, has brought into education not only methods of research but also a whole range of concepts. Let us consider the concepts of learning and development in particular. In psychology the aim is to explore the nature of human learning and development. The sense of the concepts that have come into education from psychology are influenced by this research, and the value-saturated educational concepts of learning and development tend to get suppressed; their hologramlike sense in education is made into a value-neutral process to be discovered bit by bit.

Let me try to expose my point by contrasting Piaget's psychological theory of development with either Plato's or Alfred North Whitehead's educational theories of development. Perhaps Whitehead's (1967) scheme might be better, if only to indicate that my call for educational theory doesn't require the construction of massive and complex structures but can remain quite sketchy. Whereas Piaget claims to describe what developmental changes will occur in normal social environments, Whitehead is concerned with the kind and quality of engagement individuals can have in order to approximate an educational ideal.

In Whitehead's scheme, learning is not a process whose efficiency we might want to enhance, nor is it a process about which we might expect new facts to be discovered that will enable us to educate better. Rather he sees learning and development as closely tied and sketches how they can be used to bring to life in the mind knowledge about the world. Whitehead's claims about his stages of "Precision," "Romance," and "Generalization" derive not from research into the nature of learning and development but from his conception of what it means to be educated. "Romance," for example, represents a quality of learning appropriate at certain times in mastering a discipline as well as a quality of experience one requires to become an educated person. No psychological research into the nature of learning or development could generate such a concept. It is not something that is necessary or natural, something out there that we can discover using appropriate research methods; it is a cultural artifact. Its appearance at particular times is not going to happen as a result of normal social interactions unless interactions are designed explicitly to evoke this quality, this way of seeing. Students may spend their lives at school, learning very efficiently and never experiencing the quality of romance, and they may even do better on exams than the student who has entered into romantic engagements with knowledge. But, to use Whitehead's term, in the former case the learning will remain largely "inert"—the person may become very well informed but is likely to remain "the greatest bore on God's earth" (1967, 1). We all know such people; some of us are such people.

Plato's educational scheme also has stages, which he calls *eikasia, pistis, dianoia,* and *noisis. Dianoia,* for example, is a stage more like one of Whitehead's than Piaget's. It exists only as an artifact of his general educational theory. Teaching particular subjects in a particular way brings it about. In both Plato's and Whitehead's cases, the general educational theory prescribes what stages, what parts, are required to constitute the whole, and those parts must contain within each an image of the whole.

What empirical research could usefully contribute to such theories would be to show that they are impossible; apart from that unlikely finding, it is hard to see what Plato or Whitehead might gain from empirical research on their theories.

But in the old paradigm of educational research—150 years old now—Plato's and Whitehead's are the kinds of schemes that are passed off, and passed over, as mere speculation. These speculative theories have been replaced, we are told, by a modern scientific approach that will bring scientific, or at least psychological, methods to bear on education's problems. I want to recommend looking at this with the new paradigm again, in which we can see Whitehead's scheme as indeed sketchy, but it isn't *speculation*. It isn't some kind of guess about what learning and development are that is uninformed by relevant empirical findings and consequently to be displaced by more scientific theories like Piaget's. Whitehead, on the contrary, was doing what is required of an educational theorist, generating images of the educated person and analyzing the logical entailments of such an image for teaching, learning, development, and the curriculum. Characterizing this kind of activity as unscientific speculation is only another side of the inability to recognize educational units.

Part of my problem in making this argument is due to the very great success psychology has had in taking over education. It has been so successful that even those suspicious of its influence, who also wanted to promote their own subbranch of invasion into education, seem to have been happy to negotiate a share of the invaded territory. So the philosopher R. S. Peters wanted a treaty in which philosophers and curriculum experts would deal with the subject matter, and psychologists would "have to be called in to help discover what types of content seem best suited to stimulate development from stage to stage . . . [and] what teaching methods are most effective" (1972, 128). What would Whitehead have to say to this? His stage of Romance was not something to be discovered by empirical research, nor could empirical research show how it could be deployed most effectively. Similarly, progressivism as an educational theory does not, for example, favor discovery learning methods because they are the most effective at ensuring memorization and retention of knowledge. Even if one could show empirically that they were less effective than some new subliminal drill technique, say, that finding would be beside the educational point. Progressivists favor such methods because they embody the qualities that are a part of the progressivist conception of education.

I recognize that, even to a sympathetic reading, this argument is far from conclusive and remains a bit insubstantial—relying too much on metaphors and sketchy examples—but I don't think it is entirely insubstantial. What I want to do now is move to a further dimension of doubt we might sensibly hold about the appropriateness of much empirical research to education. But I shall return to the topic of this section, by arguing that analysis of the implications of educational theories can give us many more interesting, practical, and secure results than can what is currently assumed to be the best modern scientific way to deal with educational phenomena. My first argument here is that most empirical research within this old paradigm has difficulty recognizing educational phenomena and is generally oblivious to whether its research is conducted on units of education or not. And this is how, in our educational case, problem and method pass one another by.

. . . .

THE ANALYTIC AND THE ARBITRARY

Perhaps I can try to evade mugging by adopting the role of the licensed fool for a further argument. This time I want to suggest that most empirical research in education isn't empirical in the way commonly assumed, and also that when the results of such research seem to offer guidance to education, the usefulness of the guidance results more from conceptual than from empirical features. Empirical researchers assume that their contribution to education is to expose or establish empirical connections among discrete things—such as showing effects on children's learning by use of a particular teaching method, or establishing that getting students to define their own learning goals affects their achievement, or establishing that organizing items to be learned in a particular order affects students' ability to memorize them.

The complex and messy language we have developed in our history for thinking about human behavior causes a problem for the human sciences. One result of this conceptual confusion is that it sometimes makes it hard for us to sort out whether the things between which the researcher seeks to establish empirical connections aren't already connected conceptually. To use an old and gross example, I could empirically research the question of whether all the bachelors in Vancouver are unmarried. This might involve a questionnaire and a computer to tabulate the results. I would likely be able to report as a result of my research that all the bachelors in my survey are unmarried (and that, with a 3 percent margin of error, nineteen times out of twenty, given my sample size, this result could be generalized to other bachelors in Vancouver). This finding would probably not be considered very interesting because we know that the things between which we sought an empirical connection were already tied conceptually. That is, an analysis of the meaning of *bachelor* establishes that all such people are unmarried. If I, the researcher, were to complain about your lack of interest and assert that in the past the connection had been mere speculation but that I had now scientifically established it, you would try to explain to me my confusion.

I want to argue that a great deal of empirical research in education involves the confusion of trying to establish empirical connections between things that are already conceptually tied. In most cases, of course, the conceptual connections are not as simple and obvious as the Vancouver bachelor example above, but they are of the same kind.

Jan Smedslund made this argument during the 1970s (1978a, 1978b, 1979). He analyzed various pieces of social science research and showed that they were mostly what he called pseudoempirical; they claimed to have established empirical connections when their positive findings actually relied on prior conceptual connections. Earlier A. R. Louch (1966) had shown how much research in psychology had similar defects. He began with the example of Edward Thorndike's "law of effect," which claimed to have established that people choose to repeat behaviors that have pleasurable consequences. Louch pointed out that the connection between repeating behaviors and expecting pleasurable consequences is not conceptually independent. The two behaviors are analytically tied: what we mean by choosing to repeat behaviors is tied up with what we count as pleasurable consequences. Louch further noted that E. R. Hilgard's list of findings firmly established by psychological research were similar in kind. Hilgard's first proposition was that "brighter people can learn things less bright ones cannot learn" (1956, 486). But what we *mean* by brightness involves the ability to learn more. Or take a more recent example. In the *How People Learn* project the aim has been to focus on findings that "have both a solid research base to support them and strong implications for how we teach" (Donovan et al. 1999, 12). The basic principles derived from carefully applying these criteria include the finding that: "To develop competence in an area of inquiry, students must (a) have a deep foundation of factual knowledge, (b) understand facts and ideas in the context of a conceptual framework, and (c) organize knowledge in ways that facilitate retrieval and application" (12). But (a), (b), and (c) are definitional of what we *mean* by competence in an area of inquiry. Empirical research could not have established that one could be competent in an area of inquiry without deep factual knowledge (and how deep is "deep"?), or without understanding facts and ideas in the context of a conceptual framework, or while organizing knowledge in ways that hindered retrieval and application. It may prove of practical value to spell out the meaning of competence like this, but the spelling out could have been done without the empirical research that is supposed to have established these conditions of competence.

None of these cases can be defended on the ground that science may legitimately seek to establish the obvious, and this securing of what people might often have believed or speculated can, once scientifically established, provide a reliable basis for application or further research. All the above, I am arguing, are more like trying to establish that Vancouver's bachelors are unmarried. Nor do they add precision to commonly held beliefs. This is where the arbitrary feature of much empirical research comes in. If the rock is the problem of the role of the analytic, the hard place for research in education is the arbitrariness of genuinely empirical findings.

When we do research in educational settings there is usually a fair amount of variability among the resulting data. In my story-form research, teachers employed the principles variably and students' performances varied. We know that on different days the same students perform differently and that on the same day different students perform differently. All kinds of variations come into play, and we have available techniques to use in experimental situations and techniques to use on our data that help us remove irrelevant variations.

If we were exploring how students learn and memorize information, we might run an experiment that involves the students in learning randomly ordered seven-digit numbers. If one student's randomly assigned number is her telephone number, the results of the experiment would be contaminated by this arbitrary coincidence. But a sufficiently large sample will neutralize the irregular result in this case.

Let us further assume that this experiment with learning random seven-digit numbers is part of a study that is testing the hypothesis that ordered information is more easily memorized and remembered than random or disordered information. An educational implication of supporting the hypothesis, it might be claimed, is that it will help us understand how to present information to students, particularly if we have to organize it in list form. After our experiment, and many others like it conducted with different populations, we might feel confident in claiming that our research has shown that ordered lists are learned more easily than random lists.

But you will no doubt recognize this as another of those pseudoempirical findings. The analytic component concerns the conceptual ties between order and learnability. Our minds' ability to learn and our notions of what counts as ordered are connected before and regardless of whatever research shows about their relationship. If students in our experimental group learned random lists more easily than ordered lists, we would have scanned the lists for some order we had failed to notice. On discovering that, in one case, the supposedly random number was the student's telephone number, we would feel satisfied that we had accounted for the anomalous result. What we *mean* by order is conceptually connected to what we can more readily recognize and learn. No experiment is required to establish the generalization.

In our experimental group, however, we will have had some variability among subjects' learning and memorizing the random numbers. The telephone coincidence is just one dramatic anomaly, but then there will be the case of the numbers that are, for another student, his mother's birth date, and the one that is only a digit different from another student's bank account code, and so on. Certainly not all random numbers will look equally random to all subjects. But these findings are arbitrary. We control for them by having large samples and other methods. What we cannot do, of course, is generalize from these anomalies. We cannot generalize about that student's ability to learn and memorize random numbers or about other students' ability to learn and memorize those particular numbers.

So in the case of this research we have an analytic tie that guarantees that we will establish a strong positive correlation both between orderedness in the lists and the ease of learning and memorizing and between randomness and difficulty. We have, in addition, a range of arbitrary elements that will have ensured that what counts as ordered for one subject will seem random to another, and a variety of indeterminable arbitrary contaminants in our data.

By confusing the two, by failing to distinguish the analytic component from the arbitrary components, we treat the results of our study as an empirically established connection. The analytic component, however, generalizes absolutely. The arbitrary elements cannot be generalized at all. We do not need an experiment to establish the analytic component. And the arbitrary elements, which are genuinely empirical, cannot be generalized.

Well, what range of empirical research in education is vulnerable to this critique: that its apparent empirical results are a product of confusing an analytic component and arbitrary elements? Well, quite a lot, I think. Although I have focused my attention on a form of classical empirical research that is perhaps increasingly less used, I do think that this criticism cuts a wider swathe through educational research generally. What is commonly called qualitative research, and more limited forms of phenomenological research, and other kinds — some of whose practitioners would be only to happy to cheer on a critique of standard forms of empirical research— seem to me less vulnerable to this attack. Those other methods of research, however, may be equally vulnerable to the units of education critique. Yet, having noted that, I should emphasize that many forms of empirical research evade this critique. Counting things, for one example. Counting how many times teachers address questions to boys rather than girls establishes data empirically. What such counting doesn't do is claim to establish necessary connections that expose something about the nature of our learning, development, motivation, and so on. It describes, by the old counting method, a cultural artifact or contingency and leaves us to decide what to do with the data.

Anyway, try this analysis on your favorite research, and see what you come up with.

(The example of ordered lists and learning, I might mention, is not one I chose. In my impetuous youth, a little while ago, I tried this argument out on a group of empirical researcher colleagues, taking various pieces of much-cited research as examples, showing that the positive results claimed for the research were a product of an unrecognized analytic component and greater or lesser amounts of arbitrary elements. They accused me of sneakily choosing bad research to support my argument. So I asked them to recommend a genuinely empirical finding that would be immune to this criticism, and they came up with the example used above.)

· ·

ANALYTIC FOUNDATIONS
FOR EDUCATIONAL PRACTICE

In the old paradigm, anything claimed in education without the support of empirical research is dismissed as speculative, or as the summary of the *How People Learn* project puts it, what is now "subject to powerful research tools" was in the past "a matter for philosophical arguments" (Donovan et al. 1999, 5). The implication is that cognitive science will now clear up what was formerly mere speculation or philosophical arguments, as the physical sciences cleared up, and displaced, speculation and philosophical arguments about, say, the nature of the objects visible in the night sky, the causes of diseases, and so on. I am trying to present a view of education in which empirical research in education is not like that of the physical sciences and in which what the old paradigm dismisses as speculation or philosophical arguments can be both more appropriate to dealing with education and can provide more secure and effective guidance to practice.

Let us return to the reasons why I thought my original arguments in favor of using the story-form framework for planning teaching were more secure than the research findings about its use. The framework had grown out of work I had been doing on the characteristics of children's imaginative engagements at different ages. (A peculiarity of this topic, in passing, was that everyone seemed to consider that engaging students' imaginations was very important, but I had been unable to find any research on how this might be done. I did find some research on stories, but the researchers, no doubt due to the requirements of their research methodology for a certain kind of classification of children's responses, had removed from the stories pretty much everything that gives stories their emotional power. The research was conducted with affectless event sequences, which were called "stories," and so the results did not help my search for what engages children's imaginations. Method and problem passed one another by.) Major implementation projects funded by big foundations tend to be based on what has been securely established by empirical research and thus tend to be influenced by no principle involving engaging the imagination—because there isn't a research base that could justify it.

My job here is to give reasons to believe that the old paradigm's distrust of "mere speculation," "armchair theorizing," and "philosophical arguments" and its reliance on the findings of the currently dominant forms of empirical research are flaws with serious consequences. Speculating in my armchair, I considered the universal appeal of stories. I tried to analyze what characteristics were common to those stories that were most persistently popular with children and noted that many of these features were also common to many of the corpuses of myth stories around the world. I concluded that such common features were not merely products of changing fashions but indicated something about how our minds imaginatively grasped certain kinds of material. From some amateur explorations in anthropology, poetics, and linguistics and from basic common sense, it seemed obvious that stories and their universal characteristics came along with the development of oral language—so they would appeal to all oral language users, as seemed patently the case. The precise nature of these underlying characteristics of stories, I assumed, would likely vary depending on the cultural and linguistic contexts in which they were used, even as the surface content of stories varied among linguistic groups.

For present purposes I consider just a single characteristic that emerged from this theoretical work—one common to the kinds of stories that engage young children in Western cultures. Under the surface level of, say, the Grimm folktales, we can see powerful, affective conflicts between good and bad, bravery and cowardice, compassion and cruelty, cleverness and stupidity, security and danger, and so on. Following Claude Lévi-Strauss, who had, disputably, observed such characteristics in corpuses of myth stories (1966, 1970), I suggested that these structural binary opposites are one of the features that help explain the engaging power of stories. (I elaborate this, discuss reasons for their appeal to children, and deal with a range of concerns about using such oppositions in teaching in Egan 1997, 37–44.) I then proposed that we could draw on this feature of stories in teaching mathematics, science, history, and so on.

For a brief indication of what I mean: In teaching about the properties of the air to seven-year-olds, one might organize the content on the opposites empty and full. "Empty" is represented as dull, uninteresting, boring, and "full" as rich, complex, full of wonder. We might begin by discussing how, on entering the classroom, we treat the air as empty and featureless. The unit (described in more detail in Egan 1997, ch. 8) then explores one by one the features of the air—the radio waves that throng it, the endless dust of which 60 percent is decayed human skin (an invariable "yuck!" evoker), the pollen, the microscopic life-forms, the subatomic particles shooting through from the sun, and so on. Gradually we can build up an image of the air as full, and as full of mostly invisible wonders. The elaborating story built on the affective opposition readily engages children's imaginations with the accumulating wonders of the air around them.

So we have an observation about the nature of stories, an analysis of the characteristics that give them their enormous appeal to children, the abstraction of some of these characteristics from the fictional stories and their deployment into a planning framework for teaching. But how do we know whether it will work? What if we use such binary opposites and find that children are no more engaged by them than by some other forms of teaching the same content without them? Certainly one could build a lesson on some binary opposites and have children be quite bored by it. And obviously many teachers are successful with lessons that have no hint of affective binary opposites. We did not need to do our research to recognize that some teachers will get a superficial and mechanical notion of what is required and teach exactly as usual except for occasional and apparently random references to some opposites that may be not integral to the material being taught. So what do we have from this procedure? We have a principle that, if adequately understood and deployed by the teacher, can routinely engage children's imaginations in the topics they are studying. And we have the question, how do you know?

Let's look at a further example before digging into that last question, so that we don't get too caught up with binary opposites. Among the cognitive tools that come along with literacy, I have argued (1997), is an ambivalent engagement with the extremes of experience and the limits of reality while also seeking to transcend those limits and extremes. The ambivalence finds one form in the figure of the hero, who, like us, is constrained by reality but, unlike us, seems able to transcend the constraints in some way (Frye 1957). So the twelve-year-old boy associates with the superbly skilled athlete or the twelve-year-old girl associates with the majestically powerful pop star. The imaginative engagement with the extreme works better when it can be humanized and personalized and is embedded in a narrative structure. Again, the content of our lessons in mathematics, science, history, and so on can be organized to engage and exercise these cognitive tools (as I have shown, with many examples, in Egan 1990, 1992, and 1997). At a trivial level that deals only with limits and extremes, the teacher could put on the wall for almost any topic a blank poster on which students could enter "records." These entries could take the form of the *Guinness Book of Records*, which seems to me to exploit almost ideally for males this particular cognitive tool. If the topic is the geography of Australia, for example, students might be invited to enter the name and area of the largest lake, the most dangerous insect, the longest river, the most dangerous place, the longest worm, the naturally most noisy and quiet places, the most destructive fire, and so on, and on. If the topic is invertebrate sea-creatures, we could similarly begin to build what usually quite quickly becomes an extensive knowledge base

that engages and exercises this particular cognitive tool. Less triv-
ially, we could build our topic around a transcendent human quality, seeking to evoke students' sense of wonder about some cases of
ingenuity, courage, compassion, tenacity, or whatever.

By chance, a friend, Apko Nap, who is the principal of a nearby
school, phoned me just after I had finished the previous paragraph. We have over a number of years explored ways of "narra-
tizing" teaching and learning based on such principles as are
sketched above. During the conversation he said that he would like
to read a piece from a ten-year-old boy's assignment he had received a few days ago. It concluded a study of the circulation of the
blood. The student's paper begins with an outline of the extraordinary process by which he was born as a red blood corpuscle inside
the body of Mr. Nap. We follow the spurting progress of our brave
and feisty corpuscle, which, coincidentally, had the same name as
the boy, whom I'll call Bob. Bob's life involves careening along ar-
teries with his companions and then coming to the tumult of the
heart. We follow his battering and wearying and his recognition
that his color is changing, until his journey takes him to the re-
freshing oxygen brought in by the lungs. This energizes Bob again,
and he takes us around Mr. Nap's body a few more times, describing his various tasks as he goes. A little dangerously perhaps—this
is a strict religious school—Bob notes, after another pummeling
in the heart, that Mr. Nap's pacemaker performs an important
regulatory job. The paper concludes with Bob recognizing fewer
and fewer companions on his circuit of the body and realizing
that he, too, must die. "But don't worry, Mr. Nap," he assures his
teacher, "you won't die because others like me are being born all
the time and they will carry on the vital work I did." (I quote from
memory.) The student who presents knowledge in this form must
have learned a lot about the subject and must be able to imaginatively engage with knowledge in terms of its human dimension—

exemplified in this case by a presentation that is quite touching in its conclusion.

My argument is that oral language and literacy bring along with them, or are general representations of, sets of cultural-cognitive tools. Education is properly the process dedicated to maximizing each student's mastery of cultural-cognitive tools. That is, the process of maximizing each student's cultural-cognitive toolkit encapsulates the overarching conception of education that makes mastery and exercise of particular cognitive tools units of education. Analysis of the tools leads us to methods of organizing knowledge so that it is more hospitable to being engaged by those tools and of exercising and extending them in turn. This analysis implies methods of teaching that focus on using and developing particular cultural-cognitive tools.

How can we know that organizing a lesson on invertebrate sea-creatures, or on anything else, in a narrative framework, deploying transcendent qualities, identifying limits and extremes, humanizing, and so on will lead to imaginative engagement and effective learning, and—my central claim—to a genuinely educational experience? Because engaging the imagination and making learning effective are what these cognitive tools do for human minds. Am I claiming that all children in all classrooms where such cultural-cognitive tools are deployed in shaping the lesson appropriately will enjoy these benefits? No. The degree of benefit will vary from student to student and from teacher to teacher. The causes of the variation—teaching energy that day, students' distractions by anxieties, and so on—are uncontrollable. What we have, though, is a set of principles that can guide us toward making what happens in the classroom a genuine educational experience that will, other obstacles not interfering, incidentally engage imaginations and ensure more effective learning.

Now just a minute, you might want to say. This all looks suspiciously definitional, prescriptive, and circular—there's no answer about how, empirically, we can establish any of this. That's right. In the old paradigm, the researcher who might have been patient to this point might want to say that what I have sketched here, with elaborations elsewhere, is possibly an interesting hypothesis. But that's all it is. What is now needed is empirical research that will establish whether the claims I have hypothesized are true. Until that empirical work is done, we should not take these claims seriously —they are mere speculation. My response is that what is indeed genuinely empirical—the varying degrees of benefit individual students will receive from any particular lesson—is also arbitrary; there is nothing to be established that we don't already know. There will be indeterminate interferences with students' learning and with teachers' teaching. The hypothesis is established by analysis, theoretically; human minds are engaged by these kinds of characteristics when they are embodied in knowledge. Testing that empirically would, on a much more complex level, be like trying to securely establish that all the bachelors in Vancouver are unmarried.

Well, as usual in trying to push an alternative viewpoint, this seems to be headed toward making overly rigid distinctions, suggesting that there is nothing between the analytically certain and the empirically arbitrary. And, of course, I don't mean that. There are many ways of discovering things empirically about educational phenomena that are not vulnerable to the particular criticism I am mounting here against the classic assumption underlying the more self-consciously scientific forms of educational research. The flaw I am trying to point out lies in that key assumption that human behavior has a nature that can be uncovered by application of scientific research. I obviously don't want to deny that, at the simplest level, we may observe empirical regularities in children's, schools', school districts', and principals' behavior and that we might draw implications for our future practice from such observations. Those observations need not be casual but can involve a series of research methods that are currently available. Another way of putting the problem is "that much contemporary research in psychology does not in fact have the practical implications so often claimed for it. In my view, a major reason is the tendency of psychological research, especially in the United States, to examine human mental functioning as if it existed in a cultural, institutional, and historical vacuum" (Wertsch 1991, 2).

Let me put it another way. How should we try to discover whether young children are engaged by stories? At the most basic level, we surely conclude that no experiment is required to tell us what is evident. (Even though what is evident is so as a result of our reflecting on our experience; that is, is empirical knowledge.) But perhaps research can expose what kinds of stories particular groups of children prefer? It is possible that we might learn something we don't already know from such research, but I'm inclined to doubt it. There may be some four-year-old girls or boys who, for whatever reason, don't like "Cinderella" or "Little Red Riding Hood" or "The Three Little Pigs," but the reasons are likely to reside in that realm of the arbitrary that is immune to empirical research. We get what look like useful empirical findings only if we confuse the analytic component—about children being engaged by stories—with the arbitrary component—about why certain stories appeal less or more to particular children at particular ages.

Again, I would be prudent to repeat that I don't think there is nothing between the analytically certain and the empirically arbitrary, just that we shouldn't think that we have reliable empirical research methods that will expose much of that territory to us. We have to rely on other modes of inquiry rather than assume that "Research will show that. . . ." (Also I should acknowledge the simplifications in this general argument, especially as I write this in the week of W. V. Quine's death and have implications of his celebrated paper "Two Dogmas of Empiricism" rattling around in my head.)

Empirical research, it has been assumed by very many, is the only way to establish what kind of story children enjoy and understand at different ages, for example. And, indeed, there has been interesting research of that kind conducted (for example, Applebee 1978). What kind of story children will be able to understand is only incidentally a matter of age; I am suggesting that it is primarily a matter of what cultural-cognitive tools they have acquired. That is, fluency in oral language use entails specific cognitive tools, whose appearance in stories guarantees that children will be able to understand those stories. If one includes in stories for preliterate language users some cultural-cognitive tools that only come along with literacy, then one can be confident that, to the degree that those tools play a role in the story, the story will be difficult for the preliterate child to understand.

Use of these cultural-cognitive tools in educational practice is not going to result in magic. They cannot overcome the many conditions that create resistance to learning. They are effective in that they will engage the normal child in educational activity just as reliably as "Once upon a time . . . " engages a young child or a depiction of some truly heroic event engages the twelve-year-old. We cannot know that any particular lesson or story or heroic event will engage any particular person—we cannot know all the arbitrary conditions, and knowing some will not allow us to generalize from them. Analysis of the cultural-cognitive tools that engage normal oral and literate students, however, can give us as reliable knowledge as we can find about how to go about educating them.

The way forward in improving educational practice, I suggest, will not likely result from some new facts about learning, development, or the brain—or, at least, it seems unlikely that we will learn much from such sources that can be used in educating. Rather, we might look for reliable help from more adequate—more precise, more extensive—characterizations of our acquisition of cultural-cognitive tools. We might then design more articulate ways to incorporate such tools in our teaching. That one can move from a conception of education to the cultural-cognitive tools in terms of which it is articulated to particular educational practices can give the educational administrator more security than has in the past followed the phrase "Research has shown that . . . ." In future the more reliable form may follow "Analysis has concluded that . . . ." Though we will need to be no less wary of nuttiness and dogma following such a claim.

The temptation, given the residual inclination adults typically feel toward binary categorizing, is to assert an opposite to the belief that has so long dominated educational research. And I have come close to it, suggesting that we already know enough about teaching, learning, development, motivation, and so on to get on with our educational job. But, of course, I find the psychological research into those topics quite fascinating and hope as much as anyone else, though expect less than many, that interesting new discoveries will emerge. We should not look to this new knowledge from psychological research, however, to provide us with much help with educating. Educators have been too ready to look in the wrong place for the wrong kind of knowledge to help them. It's not the lack of a "research base" of knowledge about development and learning that is hindering educators' wider success; rather, our main problem is our poverty in conceptions of education. From such conceptions we would be better able to derive developmental schemes toward educated adulthood and procedures for valuable learning. Much current educational research, viewed from this new paradigm, looks like an avoidance activity. It is looking under the psychological lamppost where it is easier to see things, rather than engaging in the harder task of generating educational theories that provide the light that can guide practice. It is always easier and more attractive to engage in technical work under an accepted paradigm than do hard thinking about the value-saturated idea of education.

Let us have more conceptions of education, then, and let us try to make those we have more elaborate and comprehensive. In *The Educated Mind*, I tried to show that we can, by climbing on the shoulders of giants and stealing their ideas, articulate a conception of education and derive from it a curriculum, an educationally relevant developmental scheme, and methods of teaching that encourage educational learning. The five categories in terms of which I articulated the overall conception of education—somatic, mythic, romantic, philosophic, and ironic—are made from the cultural stuff that education is about. They are neither implications of, nor anything one could discover from, psychological research. "Romantic" understanding, for example, builds on Whitehead's category and, even more, on Northrop Frye's analysis of romance (Frye 1957). It may, in the end, be a category to be dispensed with as not providing the most analytically fruitful way of describing a part of the educational process, but at least it provides direct access to a set of practical principles for organizing how we educate newly literate children, or adults

That is, it shows how to realize in individuals a certain conception of education. Without some such conception, all the research findings in the world are educationally blind, and with such a conception, it is unclear what research findings have to offer.

Now you might decide that the image of educated adulthood that results from acquiring somatic, mythic, romantic, philosophic, and ironic kinds of understanding is not your cup of tea. And you might conclude that Plato's *eikasia, pistis, dianoia*, and *noesis* forms of understanding don't add up to an educational ideal you share or think is possible to attain. Or you might think Whitehead's sketch of Romance, Precision, and Generalization cycles doesn't capture some aspect of your ideal of education. (Nice company I put myself in.) Decisions about your preference turn on the value-saturated business of sorting out what you think is the best way to be human, the best way to live—as Plato put it. The sad fact is that it is *only* from some such conception that we can derive educational principles.

The contribution this chapter offers toward solving the puzzle of why so many research findings seem to have had no discernible beneficial impact on education is that most of the research on learning, development, and so on is not about education.

CONCLUSION

For most of our human and prehuman ancestors' past, the mind's evolution has been a product of the codevelopment of the brain and culture. With major growths in the brain we find some evidence of greater tool use, and no doubt there were other cultural artifacts or behaviors that have not survived in any records we currently have access to. In the past sixty thousand years, with accelerating speed from about thirty thousand years ago, and with ever-increasing speed in the past three thousand years, a significant disjunction between brain and cultural development has grown. The brain's evolution continues in its purposeless and slow Darwinian way, but culture is developing in a purposeful and fast Lamarckian way—what is learned in one generation is passed on to the next. And this trick has been accelerating rapidly due to writing, in which we can record, with greater or less adequacy, our memory, experience, and thoughts and pass them to future generations. Of course, we have that natural substratum on which all cultural development rests and rides, but as Edward Skidesky has put it, "Biology has supplied us with the tools to transcend biology" (2000, 27). We have learned the trick of transcending our brain's evolutionary pace. Understanding human development is increasingly a matter of studying how culture influences and constitutes the mind.

A recent result of our cultural development is science. That is, people have worked out methods of refined observation, experiment, and inference that disclose a reliable kind of understanding of the natural world we live in. When these scientific methods are applied to the cultural world we have made, and of which they themselves are a part, they are not quite as impressive. They are good at exposing the nature of things but less good at exposing the culture of things—the human meanings of which so much of our consciousness consists. When they have been applied to trying to understand the processes involved in education, they seem less impressive still.

Discovering the nature of learning, or "the natural psychological reality in terms of which we must understand the development of knowledge" (Piaget 1964, 9), has been assumed to be the way to go to make education more effective. I have given a series of reasons why I think this has been and is unfruitful. I have also given a series of reasons for doubting or discounting the main implications this approach has yielded for educational practice.

In the alternative view I have been recommending, the education of children today is a matter of ensuring that they make their minds most abundant by acquiring the fullest array of the cultural tools that can, through learning, be made into cognitive tools. I have drawn on Vygotsky in trying to make this argument, because he more than anyone seems to me to have had an understanding of the process whereby the cultural becomes cognitive and an understanding that it is the cognitive tools we acquire that most clearly and importantly established for us the character of our understanding.

I noted in the Introduction that the central belief—the most fundamental tenet of progressivism—is that to educate children effectively it is vital to attend to the nature of the child, particularly to the child's modes of learning and stages of development, and to accommodate educational practice to what we can learn about these. I claimed that I would show that belief to be mistaken. The flaw in progressivism is the belief that we can disclose the nature of the child. Whatever is the substratum of human nature is less accessible and less useful *to the educator* than understanding the cultural-cognitive tools that shape and mediate our learning, development, and everything else to do with the conscious world of educational activity. And because all tools are not equal, we need to be guided by an overarching theory of education when conducting any educational inquiry.

Authors work hard to write in a book what they think about a topic, and obviously they work harder to make the arguments better than they casually make them in discussions with colleagues. Because some people have been very good at writing out their ideas, we tend to think of the completed book as some kind of more secure and established expression of our ideas than those casual conversations. And so it ought to be. But I think we often tend to forget how most books are made up of a set of passing thoughts that are variously in the process of changing. All this is a mumbling acknowledgment that this book is no canonical document. And by the time it is printed and in your hands, I will be curled in a corner moaning and groaning about all the things I now regret having written here and don't any longer quite believe in the way I have stated them and, worse, all the things I wish I had written. Perhaps better to see the book as merely a large and unwieldy chunk of conversation about the topics it considers. If you would like to continue this conversation, you can visit my World Wide Web home page, on which you will find a link to discussions of the topics of this book. Try www.educ.sfu.ca/people/faculty/kegan or look up my name or the book's title in your browser.

REFERENCES

Abrams, Philip. 1968. *The origins of British sociology, 1834–1914.* Chicago: University of Chicago Press.

Altwerger, Bess. 1994. In Art Levine, *"The great debate revisited." Atlantic Monthly,* 38–44.

Applebee, Arthur N. 1978. *The child's concept of story.* Chicago: University of Chicago Press.

Ausubel, David P. 1968. *Educational psychology: A cognitive view.* London: Holt, Reinehart and Winston.

Bakhurst, David, and Stuart G. Shanker, eds. 2001. *Jerome Bruner: Language, culture and self.* St. Louis, Mo.: W. B. Saunders.

Barrow, Robin. 1990. *Understanding skills: Thinking, feeling and caring.* London, Ont.: Althouse.

Beard, Charles A. 1932. Introduction to *The idea of progress: An inquiry into its growth and origin,* by J. B. Bury. London: MacMillan.

Bennett, Arnold. 1933. *The journal of Arnold Bennett.* New York: Viking.

Bickerton, Derek. 1990. *Language and species.* Chicago: University of Chicago Press.

Black, Max. 1962. *Models and metaphors.* Ithaca, N.Y.: Cornell University Press.

Bowler, Peter. 1986. *Theories of human evolution.* Baltimore: Johns Hopkins University Press.

Brainerd, Charles J. 1978. *Piaget's theory of intelligence.* Englewood Cliffs, N.J.: Prentice Hall.

Bransford, John D., Ann L. Brown, and Rodney R. Cocking, eds. 1999. *How people learn: Brain, mind, experience and school.* Washington, D.C.: National Academy Press.

Bruer, John T. 1997. Education and the brain: A bridge too far. *Educational Researcher* 26, no. 8:4–16.

Bruner, Jerome. 1986. *Actual minds, possible worlds.* Cambridge, Mass.: Harvard University Press.

———. 1990. *Acts of meaning.* Cambridge, Mass.: Harvard University Press.

———. 1996. *The culture of education.* Cambridge, Mass.: Harvard University Press.

Cazden, Courtney B. 1975. Play with language and metalinguistic awareness: One dimension of language experience. In *Dimensions of language experience,* edited by C. B. Winson. New York: Agathon Press.

Chuang Tzu. 1996. *Basic writings.* Translated by Burton Watson. 1964. Reprint, New York: Columbia University Press.

Commission on Reorganization of Secondary Education. 1918. *Cardinal principles of secondary education.* Washington, D.C.: U.S. Government Printing Office.

Cosmides, L., and J. Tooby. 1992. Cognitive adaptations for social exchange. In *The adapted mind,* edited by J. H. Barkow, L. Cosmides, and J. Tooby. Cambridge: Cambridge University Press.

Cremin, Lawrence A. 1955. The revolution in American secondary education, 1893–1918. *Teachers College Record* 56 (March):295–308.

———. 1961. *The transformation of the school: Progressivism in American education, 1876–1957.* New York: Knopf.

———. 1976. *Public education.* New York: Basic Books.

Cullingford, Cedric. 1999. *The human experience: The early years.* Aldershot, U.K.: Ashgate.

Deacon, Terrence. 1998. *The symbolic species: The coevolution of language and the brain.* New York: W. W. Norton.

Dewey, John. 1963. *Education and experience.* 1938. Reprint, New York: Free Press.

———. 1964. My pedagogic creed. In *John Dewey on Education,* edited by Reginald D. Archambault. Chicago: University of Chicago Press.

———. 1966. *Democracy and education.* 1916. Reprint, New York: Free Press.

Diamond, Jared. 1997. *Guns, germs, and steel: The fates of human societies.* New York. W. W. Norton.

Donald, Merlin. 1991. *Origins of the modern mind: Three stages in the evolution of culture and cognition.* Cambridge, Mass.: Harvard University Press.

———. 1993. Précis of *Origins of the modern mind: Three stages in the evolution of culture and cognition. Behavioral and Brain Sciences* 16:737–791.

Donovan, Suzanne, John D. Bransford, and James W. Pellegrino, eds. 1999. *How people learn: Bridging research and practice.* Washington, D.C.: National Academy Press.

Dworkin, M. S. 1965. *Dewey on education: Selections.* New York: Teachers College Press.

Duncan, D. 1908. *Life and letters of Herbert Spencer.* London: Methuen.

Egan, Kieran. 1978. What is a plot? *New Literary History* 9:455–473.

———. 1983. *Education and psychology: Plato, Piaget, and scientific psychology.* New York: Teachers College Press.

———. 1990. *Romantic understanding: The development of rationality and imagination, ages 8–15.* New York: Routledge.

———. 1992. *Imagination in teaching and learning: The middle school years.* Chicago: University of Chicago Press; London, Ont.: Althouse; London: Routledge.

————. 1997. *The educated mind: How cognitive tools shape our understanding.* Chicago: University of Chicago Press.

————. 2000. *Building my Zen garden.* Boston: Houghton Mifflin.

Elkind, David. 1981. *The hurried child: Growing up too fast too soon.* Reading, Mass.: Addison-Wesley.

Fernández-Armesto, Filipe. 1997. *Truth: A history and a guide for the perplexed.* London: Bartam.

Fodor, Jerry. 1983. *The modularity of mind: An essay on faculty psychology.* Cambridge, Mass.: MIT Press.

————. 1985. Précis of *The modularity of mind: An essay on faculty psychology. Behavioral and Brain Sciences* 8:1–42.

Frazer, James George. 1963. *The golden bough.* Toronto: Collier-Macmillan. [References are to this abridged, one-volume edition. Originally published in 12 volumes, 1890–1915.]

Frye, Northrop. 1957. *Anatomy of criticism: Four essays.* Princeton, N.J.: Princeton University Press.

Gardner, Howard. 1983. *Frames of mind: The theory of multiple intelligences.* New York: Basic Books, 1983.

————. 1991. *The unschooled mind.* New York: Basic Books.

————. 1993. *Multiple intelligences: The theory in practice.* New York: Basic Books.

————. 1997. Thinking about thinking. *New York Review of Books* (9 October):23–27.

————. 1999. *The disciplined mind: What all students should understand.* New York: Simon and Schuster.

Gardner, Howard, and Ellen Winner. 1979. The development of metaphoric competence: Implications for humanistic disciplines. In *On metaphor,* edited by Sheldon Sacks. Chicago: University of Chicago Press.

Gay, Hannah. 1998. No "heathen's corner" here: The failed campaign to memorialize Herbert Spencer in Westminster Abbey. *British Journal of the History of Science* 31:41–54.

Giles, H. H., S. P. McCutchen, and A. N. Zechiel. 1942. *Exploring the curriculum.* New York: Harper and Row.

Goldin-Meadow, S., and H. Feldman. 1975. The creation of a communication system: A study of deaf children of hearing parents. *Sign Language Studies* 8:226–236.

Goodman, Paul. 1964. *Compulsory mis-education.* New York: Horizon Press.

Gould, Stephen Jay. 1977. *Ontogeny and phylogeny.* Cambridge, Mass.: Harvard University Press.

———. 1996. *Full house: The spread of excellence from Plato to Darwin.* New York: Harmony Books.

Gross, Ronald and Beatrice, eds. 1969. *Radical school reform.* New York: Simon and Schuster.

Hall, G. Stanley. 1904. *Adolescence: Its psychology and its relations to physiology, anthropology, sociology, sex, crime, religion, and education.* 2 vols. New York: D. Appleton.

Hallam, Roy. 1969. Piaget and the teaching of history. *Educational Research* 3:211–215.

Havelock, Eric A. 1963. *Preface to Plato.* Cambridge, Mass.: Harvard University Press.

———. 1982. *The literate revolution in Greece and its cultural consequences.* Princeton, N.J.: Princeton University Press.

———. 1986. *The muse learns to write.* New Haven and London: Yale University Press.

Hazlitt, William. 1951. On the ignorance of the learned. In *A book of English essays,* edited by W. E. Williams. Harmondsworth, U.K.: Penguin.

Herriman, Michael L. 1986. Metalinguistic awareness and the growth of literacy. In *Literacy, society, and schooling,* edited by Suzanne de Castell, Allan Luke, and Kieran Egan. Cambridge: Cambridge University Press.

Hildebrand, Verna. 1981. *Introduction to early childhood education.* 3d ed. New York: Macmillan.

Hilgard, E. R. 1956. *Theories of learning.* New York: Appleton-Century-Crofts.

Hirst, Paul. 1974. *Knowledge and the curriculum.* London: Routledge and Kegan Paul.

Hofstadter, Richard. 1955. *Social Darwinism in American thought.* Rev. ed. Boston: Beacon Press.

Honan, Mark. 1981. *Matthew Arnold: A life.* New York: McGraw-Hill.

Horgan, John. 1966. *The end of science: Facing the limits of knowledge in the twilight of the scientific age.* New York: Addison-Wesley.

———. 2001. *The undiscovered mind: How the brain defies explanation.* London: Weidenfeld and Nicolson.

Housman, Laurence. 1969. *My brother, A. E. Housman: Personal recollections together with thirty hitherto unpublished poems.* 1938. Reprint, Port Washington, N.Y.: Kennikat.

Huxley, Thomas H. 1951. Natural rights and political rights. In *Nineteenth century opinion,* edited by M. Goodwin. Baltimore: Penguin.

James, William. 1890. *Principles of psychology.* 2 vols. New York: Henry Holt.

———. 1901. *Talks to teachers.* New York: Henry Holt.

———. 1978. *The works of William James: Essays in philosophy.* Vol. 5. Cambridge, Mass.: Harvard University Press.

———. 1988. *Writings, 1902–1910.* New York: Library of America.

Karmiloff-Smith, Annette. 1992. *Beyond modularity: A developmental perspective on cognitive science.* Cambridge, Mass.: MIT Press.

Kazamias, Andreas M., ed. 1966. *Herbert Spencer on education.* New York: Teachers College Press.

Kearney, Richard. 1988. *The wake of imagination*. London: Hutchinson.

Kellman, P. J., and E. S. Spelke. 1983. Perception of partly occluded objects in infancy. *Cognitive Psychology* 5:483–524.

Kennedy, James G. 1978. *Herbert Spencer*. Boston: Twayne.

Kilpatrick, William Heard. 1926. *Education for a changing civilization: Three lectures delivered on the Luther Laflin Kellogg Foundation at Rutgers University*. New York: Macmillan.

Kozulin, Alex. 1998. *Psychological tools: A sociocultural approach to education*. Cambridge, Mass.: Harvard University Press.

Kuhn, Thomas S. 1962. *The structure of scientific revolutions*. Chicago: University of Chicago Press.

Lempert, Michael P. 1997. Pragmatic constructivism: Revisiting William James's critique of Herbert Spencer. *Paideusis* 11:33–50.

Lévi-Bruhl, Lucien. 1985. *How natives think*. Translated by Lilian A. Clare. Princeton, N.J.: Princeton University Press.

Lévi-Strauss, Claude. 1966. *The savage mind*. Chicago: University of Chicago Press.

———. 1970. *The raw and the cooked*. New York: Harper and Row.

Lieberman, Philip. 1984. *The biology and evolution of language*. Cambridge, Mass.: Harvard University Press.

Locke, John. 1964. *Some thoughts concerning education*. 1693. Reprinted in *John Locke on education*, edited by Peter Gay. New York: Teachers College Press.

Louch, A. R. 1966. *Explanation and human action*. Berkeley: University of California Press.

Mandler, Jean A. 1993. A new perspective on cognitive development in infancy. In *Readings on the development of children*, edited by Mary Gauvain and Michael Cole. New York: Freeman. Originally published 1990, *American Scientist* 78:236–243.

Mandler, J. M., and P. J. Bauer. 1988. The cradle of categorization: Is the basic level basic? *Cognitive Development* 3:247–264.

Martin, Bill, Jr. 1990. An overview of a humanistic language reading program. In *Whole Language in Action,* by Nancy Polette. O'Fallon, Mo.: Book Lures.

Mehler, J., G. Lambertz, P. Jusczyk, and C. Amiel-Tison. 1986. Discrimination de la langue maternelle par le nouveau né. *Comptes-rendus de l'Académie des Sciences de Paris,* 303, 3d ser., 15:637–640.

Meltzoff, A. N. H., and R. W. Borton. 1979. Intermodal matching by human neonates. *Nature* 282:403–404.

Mithen, Steven. 1996. *The prehistory of the mind: The cognitive origins of arts, religion and science.* London: Thames and Hudson.

Moorman, Gary, William Blanton, and Thomas McLoughlin. 1994. The rhetoric of whole language. *Reading Research Quarterly* (October–December):309–329.

Morss, John R. 1990. *The biologizing of childhood: Developmental psychology and the Darwinian myth.* Hove, U.K.: Erlbaum.

Okakura, Kazuko. 1989. *The book of tea.* 1906. Reprint, Tokyo: Kodansha International.

O'Neil, P. G. 1988. Teaching effectiveness: A review of the research. *Canadian Journal of Education* 131:162–185.

Page, Norman. 1983. *A. E. Housman: A critical biography.* New York: Schocken.

Pearson, P. David. 1993. Teaching and learning reading: A research perspective. *Language Arts* 70:502–511.

Peetoom, Adrian. 1988. Publisher's Afterword to *Moving on: A whole language sourcebook for grades three and four,* by Jane Bookwill and Paulette Whitman. Toronto: Scholastic-TAB.

Perry, Ralph. 1935. *The thought and character of William James.* 2 vols. Boston: Little, Brown.

Peters, R. S. 1972. Education and human development. In *Education and the development of reason,* edited by R. F.

Dearden, P. H. Hirst, and R. S. Peters. London: Routledge and Kegan Paul.

Piaget, Jean. 1961. *Comments on Vygotsky's critical remarks.* Cambridge, Mass.: MIT Press.

———. 1964. Development and learning. In *Piaget rediscovered,* edited by Richard E. Ripple and Verne N. Rockcastle. Ithaca, N.Y.: School of Education, Cornell University.

———. 1967. *The child's conception of the world.* 1929. Reprint, Totowa, N.J.: Littlefield, Adams.

———. 1970. Piaget's theory. In *Carmichael's manual of child psychology,* edited by P. H. Mussen. Vol. 1. New York: Wiley.

———. 1971. *Biology and knowledge: An essay on the relations between organic regulations and cognitive processes.* Translated by Beatrix Walsh. Edinburgh: Edinburgh University Press.

———. 1973. *The child and reality.* Translated by Arnold Rosin. New York: Grossman.

———. 1974a. *Adaptation vitale et psychologie de l'intelligence: Sélection organique et phénocopie.* Paris: Hermann.

———. 1974b. *Understanding causality.* New York: W. W. Norton.

Pinker, Steven. 1994. *The language instinct: How the mind creates language.* New York: Morrow.

Plotkin, H. C., ed. 1988. *The role of behavior in evolution.* Cambridge, Mass.: MIT Press.

Poizner, H., E. S. Klima, and U. Bellugi. 1987. *What the hands reveal about the brain.* Cambridge, Mass.: MIT Press.

Polanyi, Michael. 1967. *The tacit dimension.* New York: Anchor Books.

Polecritti, Cynthia L. 2000. *Preaching peace in Renaissance Italy: Bernardino of Siena and his audience.* Washington, D.C.: Catholic University Press of America.

Polette, Nancy. 1990. *Whole language in action.* O'Fallan, Mo.: Book Lures.

Postman, Neil. 1982. *The disappearance of childhood.* New York: Delacorte.

Postman, Neil, and Charles Weingartner. 1969. *Teaching as a subversive activity.* New York: Delacorte.

Quick, Robert Herbert. 1890. *Essays on educational references.* 1868. Reprint, New York: D. Appleton.

Report of the Consultative Committee on the Primary School. London: Her Majesty's Stationery Office, 1931.

Rippa, S. Alexander. 1997. *Education in a free society: An American history.* 8th ed. White Plains, N.Y.: Longman.

Roldão, Maria do Céu. 1992. The concept of concrete thinking in curriculum for early education: A critical examination. Ph.D. thesis, Simon Fraser University.

Rorty, Richard. 1989. *Contingency, irony, and solidarity.* Cambridge: Cambridge University Press.

Rousseau, Jean-Jacques. 1911. *Emile.* 1762. Reprint, translated by Barbara Foxley. London: Dent.

Samuel, Hugh, and Roger Elliot. 1917. *Herbert Spencer.* New York: Books for Libraries Press.

Shaw, George Bernard. 1965. *Collected letters, 1874–1897.* Edited by Dan A. Laurence. Vol. 1. London: Max Reinhardt.

Skidesky, Edward. 2000. Where Darwin meets Malthus. *Times Literary Supplement* (18 August).

Skrupskelis, Ignas K., and Elizabeth Berkeley, eds. 1995. *The correspondence of William James.* Vol. 4. Charlottesville: University Press of Virginia.

Smedslund, Jan. 1978a. Bandura's theory of self-efficacy: A set of common-sense theorums. *Scandinavian Journal of Psychology* 18:1–14.

———. 1978b. Some psychological theories are not empirical: Reply to Bandura. *Scandinavian Journal of Psychology* 19:235–252.

———. 1979. Between the analytic and the arbitrary: A case study of psychological research. *Scandinavian Journal of Psychology* 20:101–102.

Spencer, Herbert. 1851. *Social statics.* 1850. Reprint, London: Chapman.

———. 1881. *First principles of a new system of philosophy.* 1862. Reprint, New York: D. Appleton.

———. 1888. *The principles of psychology.* Vol. 2. New York: D. Appleton.

———. 1895. *The principles of sociology.* 3d ed., rev. and enlarged. New York: Appleton. First version published, 1877; revision in three volumes: vols. 1, 2, 1886; vol. 3, 1896.

———. 1897. *The principles of psychology.* 3d ed. 2 vols. New York: D. Appleton. Considerably shorter 1st ed., 1855, supplemented in subsequent years, esp. 1888.

———. 1902. *Facts and comments.* New York: Appleton.

———. 1904. *An autobiography.* 2 vols. London: Williams and Norgate.

———. 1928. *Essays on education, etc.* Introduction by Charles W. Eliot. 1911. Reprint, London: Dent.

———. 1966a. *Herbert Spencer on education.* Introduction by Andreas M. Kazamias. New York: Teachers College Press.

———. 1966b. *Education: Intellectual, moral, and physical.* Vol. 16 of *The works of Herbert Spencer.* 21 vols. Osnabrück, Germany: Otto Zeller. Reprint of 1890 edition of *The works of H. Spencer.* Essays originally published 1854–1859.

———. 1966c. The development hypothesis. In *Essays: Scientific, political, speculative.* Vol. 1 of *The works of Herbert Spencer.* 21 vols. Osnabrück, Germany: Otto Zeller. Reprint of 1891 edition of *The works of H. Spencer.*

Sperber, Dan. 1996. Learning to pay attention: How a modular image of the mind can help to explain culture. *Times Literacy Supplement* (27 December).

Stewart, Ian, and Jack Cohen. 1997. *Figments of reality: The evolution of the curious mind*. Cambridge: Cambridge University Press.

Sugarman, Susan. 1987. *Piaget's construction of the child's reality*. Cambridge: Cambridge University Press.

Sully, James. 1895. Studies of childhood, XIV: The child as artist. *Popular Science* 48:385–395.

Thorndike, Edward L. 1913–1914. *Educational psychology*. 3 vols. New York: Teachers College, Columbia University.

Vygotsky, L. S. 1997. *The collected works of L. S. Vygotsky*. Edited by Robert W. Rieber and Jeffrey Wollock. Vol. 3. New York: Plenum.

———. 1981. The instrumental method in psychology. In *The concept of activity in Soviet psychology*, edited by J. V. Wetsch. Armonk, N.Y.: M. E. Sharpe.

Webb, Beatrice. 1971. *My apprenticeship*. 1926. Reprint, Harmondsworth, U.K.: Penguin.

Wells, Pamela. 2000. Medea or Madonna. *Times Literary Supplement* (17 March).

Wertsch, James V. 1988. *Vygotsky and the social formation of mind*. Cambridge, Mass.: Harvard University Press.

———. 1991. *Voices of the mind: A sociocultural approach to mediated action*. Cambridge, Mass.: Harvard University Press.

———. 1997. *Mind as action*. New York: Oxford University Press.

———. 1998. Mediated action. In *A companion to cognitive science*, edited by William Bechtel and George Graham. Oxford: Blackwell.

Whitehead, Alfred North. 1967. *The aims of education*. 1929. Reprint, New York: Free Press.

Winner, Ellen. 1988. *The point of words: Children's understanding of metaphor and irony*. Cambridge, Mass.: Harvard University Press.

Wittgenstein, L. 1963. *Philosophical investigations*. Translated by G. E. M. Anscombe. Oxford: Blackwell.

INDEX

Active learning, 19, 42, 43, 65–67

Analytic truth, and educational research, 64, 164–182

Applebee, Arthur, 179, 187n

Aristotle, 42, 82

Arnold, Matthew, 12, 120

Arts, in curriculum, 132–134

Ausubel, David P., 63, 187n

Autobiography, covert, in education, 123

"Back to basics," 141

Baer, Karl Ernst von, 26, 27, 84

Baldwin, James Mark, 104

Barnard, F. A., 12

Barrow, Robin, 118, 187n

Baudelaire, Charles, 102

Bauer, P. J., 96, 193n

Beard, Charles A., 8, 187n

Beecher, Henry Ward, 12

Bennett, Arnold, 11, 12, 187n

Bernardino of Siena, Saint, 149

Borton, R. W., 96, 194n

Brain: and mind, 98–101, 183

Bransford, John D., 50, 157, 188n

Brodsky, Joseph, 118

Bruner, Jerome, 157, 188n

Burgess, Anthony, 147

Carpenter, W. B., 84, 107

Carroll, Lewis, 128

Cazden, Courtney, 128, 188n

Child-centeredness, 16, 131

Chomsky, Noam, 56

Chuang Tzu, 70, 83, 112, 188n

Citizenship education, 115, 116, 135, 138, 140

Cognitive tools, 68–77, 99, 113, 174–182, 184, 185

Commission on the Reorganization of Secondary Education, 138, 139

Computers, in education, 119, 134

Concrete to abstract, 18, 43, 44, 60–65, 110

Condorcet, marquis de, 21

Creationism, 14

Cremin, Lawrence, 4, 5, 65, 97, 138, 188n

Cullingford, Cedric, 93, 188n

Curriculum, 115–148

Darwin, Charles, 14, 25, 33
Deacon, Terrence, 56, 68, 72, 100, 189n
Descartes, René, 98, 113
Development, in education, 79–114, 161–164
Developmentally appropriate teaching, 80, 105, 107, 131
Dewey, John: and development, 107–112; and learning, 48, 49, 66, 67; and precocity, 123; and social studies, 108–112, 130, 131
Donald, Merlin, 56, 84, 99, 100, 189n
Donovan, Suzanne, 155, 166, 171, 189n

Economic consequences of education, 115, 146, 147
Edison, Thomas Alva, 1
Educational research methods, 64, 65, 149–182
Eight Year Study, 140
Eliot, Charles W., 22, 122, 197n
Eliot, T. S., 111
Elkind, David, 50, 190n
Emotions, 136, 137
Evolution, 25, 37, 56, 80, 83, 85, 92

False beliefs, in childhood, 100
Fernández-Armesto, Filipe, 106, 107, 190n

Fisher Act, 139
Fodor, Jerry, 38, 39, 56, 82, 190n
Frazer, James George, 90–92, 98, 190n
Freud, Sigmund, 147
Froebel, Friedrich Wilhelm August, 13, 53
Frye, Northrop, 174, 181, 190n

Gardner, Howard, 7, 55, 58, 118, 190n
Gay, Hannah, 35, 190n
Genetic epistemology, 101
Geography, in curriculum, 109
Goodman, Paul, 5, 50, 191n
Gould, Stephen Jay, 28, 85, 191n
Grammar, teaching, 44, 53, 122, 126–129
Greek, in curriculum, 116, 132–134

Hadow Report, 139
Hall, G. Stanley, 4, 21, 27, 91, 191n
Hallam, Roy, 131, 191n
Harré, Rom, 82
Heath, Edward, 24
Helmholtz, Hermann von, 26, 27
Herbart, Johann Friedrich, 13, 53, 63
Hero, role of, in education, 174, 175, 179
Herriman, Michael, 128, 191n

Hilgard, E. R., 166, 192n
Hirst, Paul, 82, 88, 118, 192n
History, in curriculum, 107, 109,
115, 116, 129–131, 142
Housman, A. E., 119–121
Housman, Lawrence, 119, 192n
Hume, David, 42
Huxley, Thomas, 24, 32, 122, 192n

Idiots savants, 68, 69, 83
Imagination, development of, 93,
94
Infants, cognition of, 95–97, 102
Isocrates, 117

Janet, Pierre, 104

Karmiloff-Smith, Annette, 39, 57,
58, 127, 192n
Kazamias, Andreas M., 23, 192n
Kellman, P. J., 96, 193n
Kilpatrick, W. H., 49, 193n
Knowledge, as food for mind, 17,
20, 81–83, 86, 88–90, 103
Known to unknown, 62–65, 108
Kohlberg, Lawrence, 112
Kozulin, Alex, 75, 76, 113, 134, 193n
Kuhn, Thomas S., 154, 155, 193n

Lamarck, Jean-Baptiste de, 25, 33
Language, learning, 57, 58, 99

Latin, in curriculum, 115, 116, 120,
132–134
Learning, 37–77
Lempert, Michael P., 29, 39, 193n
Lenin, V. I., 118
Lévi-Bruhl, Lucien, 91, 92, 193n
Lévi-Strauss, Claude, 172, 193n
Lieberman, Philip, 56, 193n
Locke, John, 42, 116, 135, 136, 144,
193n
Losses, in developmental process,
90–94, 102
Louch, A. R., 166, 193n
Lyell, Sir Charles, 13, 14

Mandler, J. M., 95, 96, 102, 193n
Mann, Horace, 133
Marx, Karl, 44
Mathematics, teaching, 45, 49,
133
Maurier, George du, 22
Mehler, J., 96, 194n
Meltzoff, A. N. H., 96, 194n
Metalinguistic awareness, 128
Mind, coevolving with culture,
98–101, 183
Mind-body dualism, 98, 113
Mithen, Steven, 58, 194n
Modern languages, learning of,
121, 122
Modularity theories, 58, 100
Morant, Sir Robert, 138, 139, 146

Morss, John R., 81, 83, 194n
Multiple intelligences, 58

Napier, Sir Charles, 133
Nationality, 91–94, 98
Natural selection, 24, 25, 33

Oakeshott, Michael, 121
Okakura, Kazuko, 112, 194n
Oral cultures, 91, 92, 111
Ovid, 118

Paradigms, 154–182
Parker, Francis W., 4, 21, 53
Pearson, David P., 51, 194n
Pearson, Karl, 32
Peetoom, Adrian, 51, 52, 194n
Peirce, Charles S., 29
Pestalozzi, Johann Heinrich, 13,
    46, 53, 63
Peters, Richard S., 163, 194n
Piaget, Jean: and children's early
    learning, 55, 101–106; on
    development and education,
    80, 89, 94, 97–107, 161–164;
    developmental ideas in
    practice, 107–112; and history
    learning, 131; and precocity, 123
Plato, 44, 117, 144, 162, 163, 181, 182
Play, 43, 44, 141

Pleasure, as proper result of
    teaching, 19, 20, 130
Plot, of stories, 159
Plotkin, H. C., 56, 195n
Poetry, learning, 67, 68, 118
Polanyi, Michael, 69, 195n
Polecritti, Cynthia L., 149, 195n
Postman, Neil, 50, 122, 145, 196n
Potter, Kate (Lady Courtney), 32,
    33
Preconciousness, 123, 143
Progressivism: and development,
    87–97; and learning, 53–77; and
    progress, 1–7; tenets of, 5, 6, 38,
    59
Putnam, James, 29

Quick, Robert Herbert, 130, 196n
Quincy system, 52, 53
Quine, W. V., 178

Readiness, 123, 144
Recapitulation, 18, 19, 27, 28, 102,
    103, 123–126
Relevance, to student's
    experience, 140, 145, 148
Report of the Consultative
    Committee on the Primary
    School, 139, 196n
Rhetoric: in curriculum, 117;
    philosophy and, 145, 146

Roldō, Céu do, 105, 196n
Romance, in learning, 162, 181
Rote-learning, 17, 44, 67, 68, 137
Rousseau, Jean-Jacques, 8, 24, 79, 80, 89, 101, 104, 144, 196n

Science, in curriculum, 116, 121, 122
Self-education, 19, 104, 122
Simple to complex, 15, 17, 41, 60–65, 87, 110
Skidelsky, Edward, 100, 183, 196n
Smedslund, Jan, 166, 196n
Social Darwinism, 23, 24
Social efficiency, 139
Social reconstruction, 23
Social studies, 64, 107–112, 121, 130, 135, 143, 146
Social utility, in determining curriculum, 115–148
Sociology, 40
Speculation, "mere," 163, 171, 172, 177
Spelke, E. S., 96, 193n
Spencer, Herbert: character and background of, 11, 30–35; educational ideas, 13–21; ideas about curriculum, 115–125; ideas about learning, 37–47, 54, 55, 60–68, 137; influence of, 12, 21–30; influence on John Dewey, 141–145, 147;

and recapitulation, 18, 19, 125, 126
Spens and Horwood report, 140
Stories, educational uses of, 149–151, 178, 179
Sugarman, Susan, 102, 104, 198n
Sully, James, 91, 198n
Sumner, William, 24
Swan, Sir Joseph Wilson, 1

Tawney, W. H., 139
Thermodynamics, second law of, 26
Thorndike, Edward L., 4, 21, 28, 132, 166, 198n
Trivialization of primary curriculum, 60–67, 143, 148
Tyler, Ralph, 112
Tyndall, John, 26

Units of education, 158–164
Universal education, 23
Ussher, Archbishop James, 13

Vygotsky, Lev, 73–76, 113–156, 184, 198n

Webb, Beatrice, 22, 24, 26, 29–35, 46, 130, 198n
Webb, Sydney, 24

Weingartner, Charles, 122, 145, 196n

Wertsch, James, 70, 74, 76, 178, 198n

Whitehead, Alfred North, 161–164, 181, 198n

Whole language, 51–53

Whole person, education of, 16, 135

Winner, Ellen, 93, 198n

Wittgenstein, Ludwig, 156, 157, 198n